The ABC of Enneagram

Identifying the different forces that energise us

Eric Salmon

Drawings by Boss

Translated from the French by
Tanya Reznichenko and Heather Brown

First published under the title 'Les ABCs de l'Enneagramme' by Editions Grancher, Paris 1997

English translation Copyright 2003 Heather Brown

First English Edition published © 2003
by the Institute for Outdoor Learning
Plumpton Old Hall, Plumpton,
Penrith, Cumbria, CA11 9NP, UK
Tel: +44 (0)1768 885800
Fax: +44 (0)1768 885801
Email: institute@outdoor-learning.org
Web: www.outdoor-learning.org

ISBN 1-898555-08-7

The Institute for Outdoor Learning (Charity no. 1085697)
The Institute for Outdoor Learning supports, develops and promoted learning through outdoor experiences.

IOL believes in the value and importance of outdoor learning and, as a professional association, promotes ethical and sustainable use of the outdoors among outdoor learning professionals. IOL's many activities include membership services and support, lobbying, publications, conferences, special interest groups and the development of regional activities.

Typeset by the Institute for Outdoor Learning
Printed by Fingerprints, Barrow-in-Furness, UK.

To Augustin, my son.

Also to Helen, David and Peter, and with
thanks to Heather, Tanya, Ann, Michael,
Paul, Martin, Henk and Jeanette.

From the Author to the Reader

The Enneagram is an aid that enables us to illustrate the great truths of human nature.

We have chosen to stay as close as possible to real life by building this book around personal accounts and real life stories, using animals to help bring the descriptions to life. In doing this, we have a precedent in Aristotle and La Fontaine, who both used animal imagery to aid self-knowledge. They showed that being a little humorous need not be incompatible with a great respect for human nature, in fact, it's just the opposite. It is in this spirit that the illustrations for this book were created.

Some definitions:
The word passion is used here in its original meaning:

Passion: a violent desire or irresistible leaning, which tends to become the centre of the soul's life, to the exclusion of other things'.[1]

Fixation: attachment to specific means of satisfaction, to the point of no longer being able to free oneself from it.

Behaviour: manner of acting, or conducting oneself.

Ego: interest that the self takes in itself.

Psychology: literally, *psycho logos*, the word of the psyche.

Psyche: 'The human mind or soul. In Greek myth, a girl loved by Eros (Cupid), who became the personification of the soul.'[2]

A Note on the Translation

Besides the wonderful pictures, one of the reasons I found this book interesting is because it was originally written in French, from a French perspective. In the translation, I have tried to keep the flavour of the original, so if sometimes a turn of phrase seems a bit strange, I invite you to consider what extra dimension it might bring to the description; if it's not clear, please let me know!

Heather Brown

---

[1] Merriam-Webster's Collegiate Dictionary, 2000
[2] Collins English Dictionary, Millennium Edition

Contents

Introduction

What is the most important thing in life? Of course we all need food, love and tenderness, but there is another thing we all need: to know who we are.

Jostein Gaardner (1995), *Sophie's Choice*

One good reason for talking about self-knowledge is the malaise that pervades our world, which comes from a lack of personal responsibility. In the past, we let the banker take care of our money, the doctor take care of our body, and the confessor was in charge of looking after our soul. But those days are over. Today, we need to take personal responsibility for the management of our savings, of our body, and of our psychological health. To do this, we need reference points.

Relationships have always fascinated me and, in order to provide a framework for my knowledge, I was looking for a simple tool to help me understand others in depth. I wanted to know 'Who are these friends I rub shoulders with every day, behind their external shell? How can I appreciate their truly beautiful inner selves, behind their masks?'

Experience has taught me that knowledge of other people has to begin with self-knowledge. Now that's a much more difficult challenge! It doesn't take much thought to realise that we are made up of a cacophony of little selves who live together for better or worse, often ruled by our emotions.

This is where I first found the Enneagram useful; it names and identifies these different facets of ourselves. Starting from each dominant characteristic, it offers us nine patterns of coherent psychological structure. In this way, the Enneagram offers us some basic principles that can help us to understand the inner workings of human nature.

Later, I realised that we are all interested in personality. I'd like to bet that we've all filled in a personality test in a magazine at some point, and that we have all said at some time or other, of a spouse or child: 'I will never understand them!'

In my search for a tool to simplify my understanding of our 'inner machine,' I instantly appreciated the clarity and dynamics of the Enneagram. But its greatest gift is to make us appreciate the budding radiance of all those we meet. Clearly, we are potentially much more beautiful than we believe ourselves to be.

This book was born out of my desire to share this gift.

PART ONE

What is the Enneagram?

*Do I really exist? ...Isn't there a Greater Self, true and free,
beyond my little illusory self? Isn't there a better way to
live, and a means to reach this higher state?*

Louis Pauwels, *Monsieur Gurdjieff*

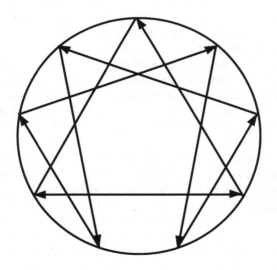

What is the Enneagram?

The word 'Enneagram' comes from the Greek *ennea gramma*, which means 'nine-sided figure.' Today, this word refers to a system of personality study based on nine types of human behaviour.

Historically, it is based on key character traits that are found in many traditions and cultures, on both the spiritual and philosophical level, such as the Buddhist wheel of life or the Christian seven deadly sins. These character traits, also called 'passions,' are kinds of unconscious conditioning that influence our behaviour. In the Enneagram, there are nine of them: anger, pride, deceit, envy, avarice, fear, gluttony, lust, and sloth.

The Enneagram is rich because it considers the dynamics of human nature, our evolution and the different facets of our personality. It is concrete because it applies to everyday habits, so, if we combine it with good self-observation, it is instantly useful. It is credible because the types are compatible with observable data, including those that underpin modern psychology.

The main idea of the Enneagram is based on the principle that we all have a central character trait, like an axis around which our personality turns. This 'fixation' relates to a defence mechanism put in place when we were children. This fixation – which is usually unconscious – plays out in our everyday habits and limits our world view.

In psychological terms, the Enneagram invites us to recognise the fact that our personalities have frozen us into this conditioned behaviour. The Enneagram also gives us reference points so that we can free ourselves from the influence of this conditioned self, which we call the ego.

On a spiritual level, the challenge is to find the deep essence that lives inside us, beyond our personality. Like other typologies used for spiritual development, understanding our Enneagram 'type' can be seen as a starting point for change, the axis of transformation through which ordinary consciousness can evolve toward dimensions of higher being.

The Enneagram is instantly accessible because it deals with the central preoccupation of each type, names it and offers us ways of observing ourselves, so that we can recognise the point to which the passion has infiltrated our lives. It therefore has immediate value, because if we know what we are looking for, it can help us to understand a lot about how we operate. The aim of all this is to help us to heal ourselves, through knowing ourselves better.

The Enneagram has connections back not only to the Christian and Sufi traditions; it also has analogies to the Hebrew Kabbalah's Tree. Many great names seem to have been involved with the history of the Enneagram: Pythagoras, Dante, Gurdjieff. Pythagoras, who was born on the Greek island of Samos, and who lived for thirty years as an expatriate at Thebes and Babylon, was fascinated by the human soul. We can trace the history of the diagram back to 600 BC. It was the ninth of Pythagoras' ten seals.

On the pediment of the temple of Apollo at Delphi was written: 'Know yourself, and you will know the universe and the gods'. In antiquity, psychology was closely tied to philosophy and religion. This relationship between the different human sciences has since been lost, especially in the 20th century.

Today, it seems that the notion of the psychospiritual is being reborn. In fact, more and more processes are trying to connect psychological development with spiritual growth, self-knowledge with the transformation of being, the world of the soul with that of the spirit. This is what the Enneagram does.

The process of self-development is the same whatever the culture it operates in: Self-knowledge, Transformation, Fulfilment. Self-knowledge is the starting point, transformation is the way, and fulfilment is the goal; the aim is to contact our deep essence, the power of life that can energise us if we can let go of our ego, the part of us that believers call the soul.

The Enneagram can help us to carry out these three stages of the process:
- In terms of self-knowledge, it gives us the keys to who we are.
- In terms of transformation, it is like a guide, a map of the psyche that gives us clear directions...but it can't do the work for us!
- As for the essence of being, that is what the Enneagram is all about; it is both the end and the means of our development.

Right thought or right action has a special flavour. People who have learned to recognise it can tell whether their thoughts or acts are centred in the present or if they are somewhere else, conditioned in their patterns. This is nothing new, but the Enneagram can help us notice this more clearly.

The journalist and writer Michael Goldberg (1994) feels that:
By becoming conscious of our mode of attention, we discover how our worldview is limited, and how it differs from those of others. We see how their journeys, their personal experiences are different; we begin to understand their point of view. We also discover that others share the same perspective as us, and we then begin to understand the meaning of the word 'compassion,' both for ourselves and for others.

Since 1990, the Enneagram has developed quickly across the world. It has two great practical uses: making daily life easier, and finding unity in oneself and with one's environment.

The personality types are only a tiny part of the teaching of the Enneagram. In this introductory text, we focus on psychological structure and some historical facts.

The Diagram of the Enneagram

The Enneagram is represented by a nine-pointed star inside a circle. It is made up of three elements:

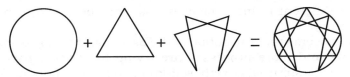

-a circle
-an equilateral triangle
-an irregular six-sided figure called a hexade

The points of the triangle and of the hexade together form nine equidistant points around a circle.

The nine points of contact between the circle and the nine-pointed star represent the bases of the nine personality types. The diagram is rich in symbolism; unfortunately we don't have the space here to explore that side of the Enneagram.

The circle

The circle symbolises the Whole, perfect unity.
The circle also represents the inter-connectedness of our psyche.
The nine points are landmarks that enable us to shed light on the darkness of the inner labyrinth of our mind.
We all have each of the nine points inside us.

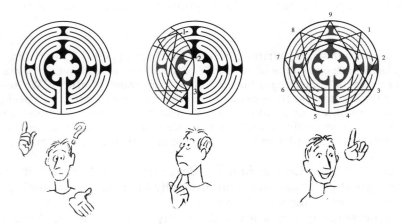

We can use the Enneagram to better understand the labyrinth of our psyche.

The ABC of the Enneagram

The nine points of the Enneagram also represent the contradictory forces that we have inside us. The aim of working with the system is to try to recognise and rebalance these forces. Each of the nine forces has been given a name. The arrows represent the interactions between these forces.

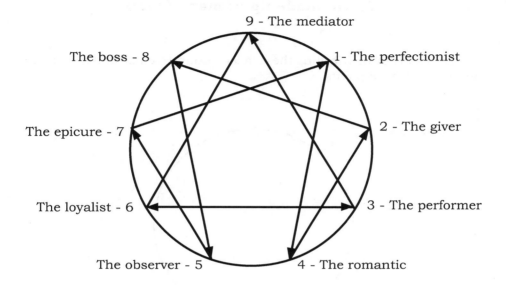

The Enneagram represents the different components of our psyche. To make identification easier, a name and number has been given to each of them.

Each of us has a dominant point or type. The second part of this book is dedicated to the study of the nine personality types, each of which corresponds to a dominant characteristic. Of course, the millions of people who identify themselves as, for example, 'Type Two: predominantly a giver', are all different, because we all have all nine of these forces within us to varying degrees. However, what people who recognise their passion as Two have in common, is that their psychic functioning is similar.

How the Enneagram works in Everyday Life

We are made up of many facets

Let's start by distributing these facets around a circle and recognising the nine reference points.

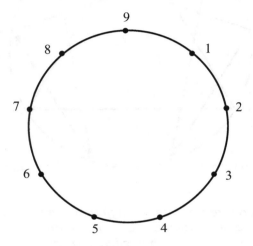

The circle represents the whole of our psyche. The nine bases are reference points representing the principal forces that drive us.

In order to see how these forces play out in everyday life, let's look at an example:

Example 1

I've just remembered that Mother's day is in 2 weeks. My different little selves are arguing with each other and giving their opinions about what to do. This generates, in no particular order:
- I have to find a present. It's a matter of principle.
- I've got an original idea: a silk scarf.
- Not bad, that'll be useful for her, and it'll express the warmth and affection I feel for her.
- OK, stop hesitating, we need to decide right now.

- Let's think about this calmly: how many scarves does she have? What do they look like?
- That's not important. This one will be new, and the colours are cheerful!
- I'm pretty sure she needs one. It would be practical and effective.
- Yes, but I'm afraid of giving her something she already has!
- Why hurry? I'd like to take some time to choose in peace.

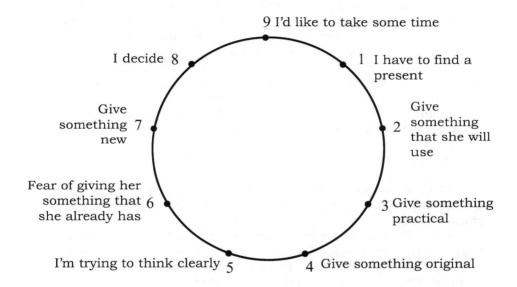

9 I'd like to take some time

I decide 8

1 I have to find a present

Give something 7 new

2 Give something that she will use

Fear of giving her something that 6 she already has

3 Give something practical

I'm trying to think clearly 5

4 Give something original

Example 1. Mother's Day:
nine facets are arguing inside me.

Comments on Example 1

At any given moment, a number of facets of ourselves are talking to each other. Different forces are pulling in different directions. In theory, we lucidly choose whichever facet or behaviour is most appropriate at that moment. But in fact, practical experience proves that most of the time we tend to focus on one facet at the expense of the others.

The ABC of the Enneagram

The same facet often dominates

Example 2

A group of friends meet in a bar after a football game on a Sunday night. Let's see how different their feelings are about the same experience.

Tony: I'm happy with my game. We didn't win but I played better than last time. I had the rulebook in my pocket, so we could check straight away which rule we needed to apply to each incident.

Daniel: It was a very emotional day, because it was the first time that Paul played since his accident.

Bart: I'm happy with my game. I'm not bothered about how I played, but because I always have surgical tape on me, I was able to help our opponents when they were injured.

John: They were good. We had to fight to the end. I like it when we have good strong opponents. I also made several really good passes.

Manny: I was happy being on the bench. I enjoyed watching the tactics of both teams.

Gary: Although we lost, I had a good time. It was great; there were new people, the weather was nice, and Victor had lots of funny stories to tell.

Carl: We lost and we didn't even score a goal. I live for winning. I can't enjoy myself when I lose.

Kim: I thought they were going to be good, and my concern was justified. They were better than I anticipated.

Larry: It was just good that we were all together, the end result doesn't matter.

The ABC of the Enneagram

Comments on Example 2

Our nine friends interpreted the same information differently.

We all have filters of perception that direct our attention to certain aspects of a situation rather than others. If we take a step back and examine our habits, we will notice the extent to which our behaviour is conditioned, according to the facet we focus on.

If we went to this bar several times, we would notice that the same characters tended consistently to be interested in the same subjects: some focusing on respecting the rules, others on winning, others on novelty...

The Enneagram helps us to answer the question: 'What is my dominant characteristic?' Once we've recognised that, we can then start to see how these different forces that make up our personality coexist.

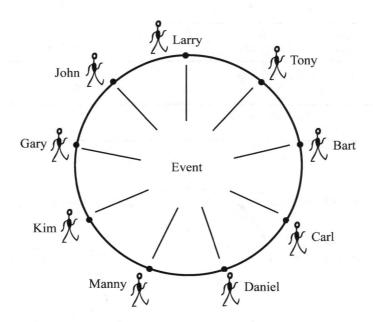

Nine witnesses of the same event experienced the same thing, but filtered the information in different ways.

We are proud of this dominant facet

We are more or less set in the way we interpret events. We tend to focus on aspects of the situation that confirm our value system.

Let's return to our Mother's Day example:

Expression	Related Facet
I have to find a present. It's a matter of principle.	Respect for customs
I have an original idea: a silk scarf.	Creativity, originality
Not bad, that'll be useful for her, and it'll express the warmth and affection I feel for her.	Consideration for other people
Ok, stop hesitating, we have to decide right now.	Power of decision
Let's think about this calmly: how many scarves does she have? What do they look like?	Reasoning, clarity
That's not important. This one will be new, and the colours are so cheerful!	Novelty, cheerfulness
I'm pretty sure she needs it. It will be practical and effective.	Efficiency
Yes, but I'm afraid of giving her something she already has!	Doubt
Why hurry? I'd like to take some time to choose in peace.	Harmony

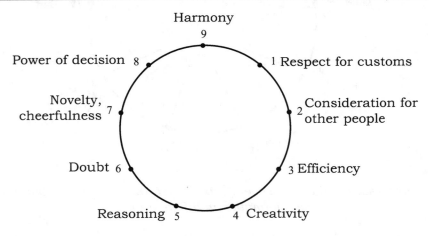

Example 1: Different facets express themselves inside me

The ABC of the Enneagram

Now let's go back to the bar example:

Expression	Related Facet
Tony: I'm happy with my game. We didn't win but I played better than the last time. I had the rulebook in my pocket, so we could check straight away which rule we needed to apply to each incident.	● Respect for the rules and integrity
Daniel: It was a very emotional day, because it was the first time that Paul played since his accident.	● Emotions, whatever is out of the ordinary
Bart: I'm happy with my game. I'm not bothered about how I played, but because I always have surgical tape on me, I was able to help our opponents when they were injured.	● Consideration for others, being helpful
John: They were good. We had to fight to the end. I like it when we have good strong opponents. I also made several really good passes.	● Power, strength
Manny: I was happy being on the bench. I enjoyed watching the tactics of both teams.	● Detachment, cool reasoning
Gary: Although we lost, I had a good time. It was great; there were new people, the weather was nice, and Victor had lots of funny stories to tell.	● The bright side of things
Carl: We lost and we didn't even score a goal. I live for winning. I can't enjoy myself when I lose.	● Success, efficiency
Kim: I thought they were going to be good, and my concern was justified. They were better than I anticipated.	● Doubt
Larry: It was just good that we were all together, the end result doesn't matter.	● Harmony

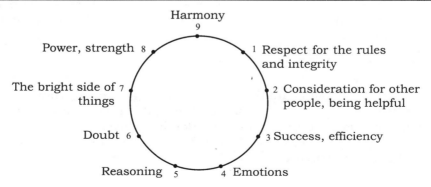

Example 2: Different personal experiences of the same situation.

Our habits are connected to our value system

Example

Tony, for whom law and order and honesty are important, has 'respect for the rules' as a filter of perception. Unconsciously guided by that, Tony has habits like: being afraid to make a mistake, judging in terms of right or wrong, working by the book, being conscientious, tidy, and demanding...

Tony exemplifies the habits of type One:
predominantly a perfectionist

They are afraid of
making a mistake

...For them, you're
either right or wrong...

Meticulous, they work
by the book

They are
conscientious
and tidy

They have a high
moral sense

They are demanding,
but they rarely get
angry

All these habits are the reflection of single facet in Tony: 'respect for the rules and morals'. This view of things, this system of values based on honesty, relates to the Enneagram dominant passion of Perfectionist. If Tony only uses this part of himself, he only uses one part of his potential, as the following figure shows:

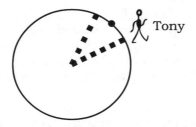
Tony

Tony focuses on respect for rules: by having one view of things, one system of values, he focuses on only one part of reality.

Tony's example holds true for the eight other characters we met in the bar, as we will see in Part 2.

We are free

At any point in our lives, we can choose to get stuck in our view of things or to open up other possibilities for ourselves. Thus, still using the same example, Tony might at any point:

Get stuck and become:	*Open himself up to his other facets:*
uncompromising, obsessive, fussy, fanatical, set in his principles.	Focused on making justice prevail, honest, rigorous, upholding the natural order of things.

Dispensing justice set in his convictions

Dispensing justice in serenity

In those two manifestations of type, the underlying values are the same, but their expression is different. So there isn't a good type or a bad type, just different ways of living out the characteristics of our personality. Sometimes we get stuck in our point of view; at other times we are able to see the wider scheme of things, although we still see the world through the same dominant facet.

The nine passions have ancient origins

These nine dominant personality features correspond to nine historic facets, which are first found in the work of the Desert Fathers in the 4th century. They appear again in Dante's *The Divine Comedy* in the 14th century, and Oscar Ichazo placed them on the Enneagram diagram. (see Part 4: The History of the Enneagram)

The nine Passions: historical development

Type	The Desert Fathers (4th century)	Dante The Divine Comedy (14th century)	Oscar Ichazo (1970)
1	Anger	Anger/Meekness	Anger/Serenity
2	Pride	Pride/Humility	Pride/Humility
3	Vanity	-	Deceit/Truthfulness
4	Envy and sadness	Envy/Charity	Envy/ Equanimity
5	Avarice	Avarice/Poverty	Avarice/Detachment
6	-	-	Fear/Courage
7	Gluttony	Gluttony/Abstinence	Gluttony/Sobriety
8	Lust	Lust/Chastity	Excess/Innocence
9	Sloth	Sloth/Zeal	Laziness/Action

Each of the nine points has two extremes: passion and virtue. The credibility of the Enneagram also comes from close analogies between the passions and the description of personality disorders.[3]

---

[3] See *the Diagnostic and Statistical Manual of Mental Disorders, DSM-IV*, American Psychiatric Press, 1994. The corresponding personality disorders are as follows: obsessive compulsive (1), histrionic (2), borderline and depressive (4), avoidant and schizoid (5), paranoid (6), narcissistic (7), anti-social (8), dependent and passive aggressive (9).

The ABC of the Enneagram

The nine Passions

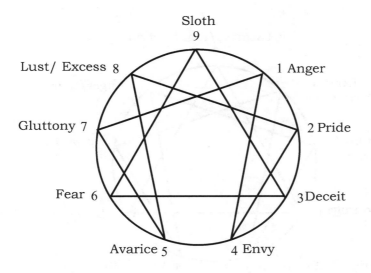

The nine Virtues

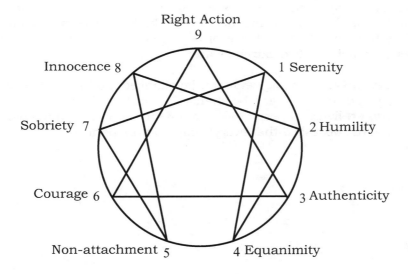

Thus each of the points corresponds to a passion and a virtue.

The nine points and the passion/virtue relationship

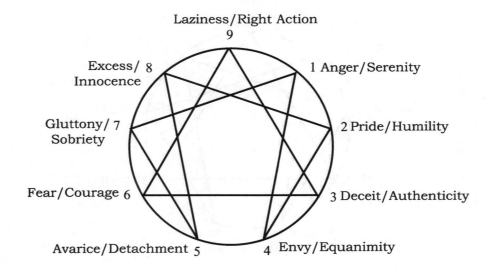

Coming back to Tony as our example, let's imagine that he is under the influence of his Perfectionist dominant characteristic, so the breaking of rules annoys him, and his anger rises every time he notices an imperfection. He is operating therefore at the Anger/Serenity point, which means that he has the choice of coping with his resentment in many ways, of which the two extremes are:

Serenity: changing what can be changed, and staying serene in the face of what can't be changed

Anger: living in perpetual resentment about everything which is not ok: obsessed that everything must be perfect.

The ABC of the Enneagram

Our value system is tied to our perception of the world in childhood

In the beginning, we were all Everything. One approach to psychology considers that, at the moment of birth, the child has free access to all possible behaviours[4].

Then, confronted by the world, we develop a protective mechanism, a strategy to enable us to best adapt to our environment. Since this strategy is eminently reassuring, we choose to repeat it to the point where we use it exclusively, to the detriment of other possible strategies. This recurring behaviour is our personality. As adults, we spend most of our time set in our point of view; we continue to live with our defence mechanisms, with protective shells that unconsciously reassure us, but which prevent us from developing the whole of our possibilities. The bulk of our potential remains uncultivated.

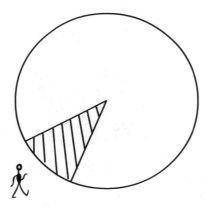

Generally, we only use a part of our potential

---

[4] This view of things also corresponds to that of Pythagoras, and the spiritual world in general, for which the soul, at the moment when it is incarnated in the body of the child, is naturally in contact with God, with the Whole. The nine points of the Enneagram represent nine colourations of this divine essence. Each of them corresponds to one of a certain number of characteristics called talents. The main difference is that, in this more spiritual view of things, it is generally considered that the soul has chosen in advance the most appropriate context for its development. Individuals are therefore born with the most appropriate personality for their path of evolution.

Example 3

If my first (usually unconscious) perception of the world is of being invaded in my personal space, I will live my life putting a distance between myself and others in order to protect myself. This inheritance from childhood generates a number of attitudes that can be observed in my habits.

Perception of the child:
→ 'The world is intrusive'.
Unconscious defence mechanism:
→ 'I have to protect my privacy'.

Therefore, in everyday life my behaviour will tend towards searching for privacy, being autonomous, understanding how things and people function in order to be prepared for their arrival...
You will be able to see this repeated behaviour in my everyday habits.

Fives are observers, loners who are concerned about their personal space.

They are independent.

...self-sufficient.

They are logical and analytical.

They like to understand, have the big picture...

Observing rather than participating.

Habits of Type Five, the Observer

The ABC of the Enneagram

Psychologist Margaret Frings Keyes describes it this way[5]:

> Each of the nine essential patterns reflected by the Enneagram represents a basic survival strategy and an appropriate response to the child's life circumstances. This point of view, like a window through which one glimpses only a part of reality, leads the child to interpret events during the rest of his or her life in this light. The child identifies with the small window frame of reference.
>
> Children need protection while they take the risks they need to grow. Otherwise they can be easily overwhelmed and develop rigid behaviors to protect themselves.
>
> When we reject or do not see other points of view, we behave automatically from a defense-conditioned framework, somewhat like a robot or as if half asleep. Basic goals of human behavior – survival, pleasure, and relationships – become distorted. We pursue them in fixated shadow ways, contaminated with excessive desire and hatred. Thus, we all have a characteristic distortion, based on what was missing or what we gave too much importance to in early childhood.

---

[5] *The Enneagram Relationship Workbook*, Molystandur Publications, 1992.

We can summarise this idea by this diagram:

Everyone has central character trait, like an axis
around which their personality turns

↕

This fixation corresponds to the defence system
put in place by the child.

↕

This fixation is usually unconscious. It plays out
in our everyday habits.

↕

It limits our vision of the world to our own way
of seeing things.

↕

The Enneagram represents nine points of view.
Each of the types corresponds to one of these passions.

We can look at it like an iceberg:

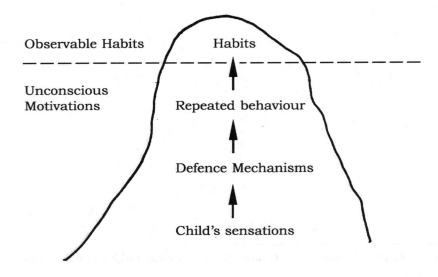

Observable Habits   Habits

Unconscious
Motivations   Repeated behaviour

↑

Defence Mechanisms

↑

Child's sensations

The ABC of the Enneagram

The Dynamics of the Enneagram

Everyone in the world is situated somewhere around the Enneagram circle. Our position on the circle depends on the dominant element of our psyche. The personality types described in the following chapters are true for people who are situated precisely on each point. The Enneagram invites us to find our own place on the circle, and the descriptions of the habits are designed to help us do this.

Just as our first perception of the world never changes, our type doesn't change. But the Enneagram takes into account other variables:

1- The wings

The first variable concerns our location on the circle. We can be more or less close to a base point.

Example:

On reading the descriptions of different base types, Carol locates herself on both type Six and type Seven. Therefore, Carol probably has either a base Seven, influenced by her wing Six, or a base Six influenced by her wing Seven.

On the Enneagram, Carol's position is called Type Seven with a Six wing.

2 - The arrows

They show us the other 'little selves' which we use frequently in our behaviour. The Enneagram defines two situations where we abandon the filtering mechanisms that we use most of the time: stressful situations and safe situations.

When we are in the quiet of our home, we tend to relax and behave differently from the way we behave out in the world. Equally, in a stressful situation, for example, the week before an exam, we (consciously or unconsciously) modify our habits in order to face up to this event.

Let's go back to our example of Tony, who is located on base One. Tony, in a safe situation, spending an evening with friends for example, may well relax his usual strictness, and will allow himself to look more on the bright side of things, an attitude associated with point Seven.

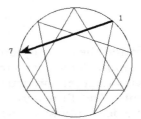

Tony, who normally behaves according to the habits of point One, changes his behaviour in safe situations and takes on the characteristics of point Seven.

In a stressful situation, when Tony realises that complete perfection is unattainable, emotions other than his usual resentment will emerge. Tony will shift to his Four facet. His emotions have became so strong that they need to find expression, so he can either let himself go into disappointment or depression 'Nobody loves me', or he can transform this emotional energy into creativity, finding ideas that he never would have had by staying stuck in his base One.

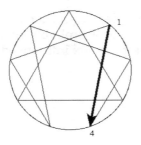

Tony, who normally behaves according to the habits of point One, changes his behaviour in stressful situations and takes on the characteristics of point Four.

The ABC of the Enneagram

These two arrow directions also give us ideas about behaviours that can help our development. If we locate ourselves in one base type, the arrows will show us which other behaviours are most easily accessible to us. The directions of the arrows show where each type goes in stressful situations.

Thus each one of us has four principal facets: the base, the neighbouring type called the wing, and the influence of the two arrows. If we take time to observe our behaviour, the Enneagram will enable us to understand how our inner facets interact and play out in our lives. Understanding these relationships also enables us to understand how the different Enneagram points relate to each other. Recognising your type means naming your dominant ego, so that you can start to transform passion into virtue.

Summary

Each one of us has a main filter of perception that unconsciously directs our life, and even determines our way of thinking.

This filter of perception didn't develop by accident; we developed it to protect our essence or true Self, and our personality developed around this protective mechanism. This strategy was useful in childhood, but it is no longer helpful as an adult; it blinkers our perception and limits our choices. However, this unconscious motivation did enable us to develop certain good qualities associated with our recurrent behaviour. We became exceptionally gifted in the characteristics of our type.

Thus, finding our base point shows us at the same time our main shortcoming and our greatest potential. The finest expression of these qualities becomes possible when we can tame our ego, which means getting out from our automatic filter of perception, in order to act consciously.

The key points of this chapter

Main principles

- We are made up of many facets.
- The same facet (or type) is often dominant.
- We are proud of this dominant facet.
- Our habits are developed because of what we value.
- We can choose to stay stuck in our type or to open ourselves to other possibilities
- The nine dominant features of personality have ancient origins
- Our value system is based on our childhood perception of the world
- Our dominant type is influenced by three other types.
- Recognising our type provides a starting point for the transformation of the ego.

Main characteristics of the Enneagram

- It brings together a diagram and the study of personality.
- It relates to and describes our daily habits.
- It explains what's behind our behaviour.
- It is universal: it's valid for all people, of all ages and of all countries. For a number of years now, it has been taught in many countries around the world.
- It is dynamic. It takes into account:
  - the different facets of each person
  - the potential evolution of each person
  - free will
- It can be used to guide our psychological development and/or our spiritual evolution.

Who is interested in the Enneagram?

The spiritual community

The world of business, business schools

The psychological establishment

Individuals in their private life: relationships, children's education

Individuals in their professional life

Individuals in their spiritual development

The Enneagram is taught in several universities, particularly Stanford in the USA, as part of courses in psychology, psychiatry and medicine.

Business schools have adopted it to teach human resource management. Businesses use it in order to deepen human relationships.

What is the Enneagram used for?

- Providing reference points for understanding personality: starting points for understanding our own behaviour and that of people close to us.
- Knowing ourselves, identifying our potential: sorting out the many facets of personality.
- Recognising that an unconscious motivation exists, an axis, an orchestral conductor who directs our behaviour.
- Understanding others in depth: seeing them as they really are, from their point of view, and not as they appear to be.
- Gaining depth in our human relationships.

- Transforming ourselves:
  - Structuring our personal development.
  - Developing self-observation.
  - Realising our potential: converting passion into virtue or rediscovering the unifying principle in the multiple forces that drive us.

PART TWO

Introducing the Nine Personality Types

The man is much to be pitied who knows not how to laugh at himself.

Voltaire

Understanding Personality using the Enneagram

The oral tradition

Each one of us is a living, unique person. Right from its beginnings in the ancient past, the teaching of the Enneagram was done orally, in order to honour and protect these two dimensions. And that is still true today.

Helen Palmer was also concerned to preserve these values, and created a method of teaching that she called the oral tradition, which aims to transmit the knowledge of the Enneagram through real life examples. Enneagram teachers in the oral tradition believe that the best way to learn about the Enneagram is through a workshop, where, in a spirit of immense respect for each personís uniqueness, you can listen to each otherís experiences. Participants who have discovered their type come to talk about their experiences, in order to illustrate the characteristics of their type.

We too want to be faithful to this tradition; we believe that the Enneagram has to be based on real life and not on theories. It's in this spirit that we have put together the second part of this book, which is based on stories and comments made by participants in our own workshops. Their comments and stories are shown in italics.

How to approach exploring and recognising our type

This involves an extremely challenging task, because we need to accept that, for many years, we have been under the influence of an unconscious motivation that directs our life. Some people spend their entire lives trying to decode their inner functioning.

The fact that the Enneagram can help us do this, doesn't take away from the fact that sorting out who we think we are, who we would like to be, who we would have liked to have been, and who we really are, will demand rigour and honesty, but above all, time.

It is important to remember that what we are today is the result of setting up protective mechanisms that were indispensable in our earlier life. This is neither good nor bad. Moreover, if you recognise yourself in several Enneagram points, that is a perfectly normal stage to go through. The most important thing isn't so much fitting ourselves into the system, but being honest and authentic as we journey towards seeing more clearly what is inside us.

Close friends and family can generally give good advice to help us discover who we really are. In addition, we can ask ourselves which behaviour we were closest to at the age of about twenty, as the characteristics of our dominant type are generally very distinct at that age.

If we recognise ourselves in several dominant characteristics or Points, it can be helpful to remember that our Enneagram type is the product of several facets, which we described in the previous chapter. For example, if we find ourselves in bases Three and Four, we may be located between the two. The same reasoning applies if we find myself on two points connected by arrows. For example, certain people in base Five can associate with their Point Seven so often that in the beginning they find it hard to know which one is dominant.

Recognising our ego, our dominant Point, our passion, is the departure point for transforming our being. As we will see later on, once we have recognised our base type, we use that knowledge for personal development. But before we can transform anything, we first need to understand what raw material we are working with.

The type descriptions

Each personality type bears the name of its dominant self, and a number, and we will look at them in this order:

Point One: predominantly a Perfectionist
Point Two: predominantly a Giver
Point Three: predominantly a Performer
Point Four: predominantly a Romantic
Point Five: predominantly an Observer
Point Six: predominantly a Loyalist
Point Seven: predominantly an Epicure
Point Eight: predominantly a Boss
Point Nine: predominantly a Mediator

In the descriptions, we focus on the uniqueness of each type: how it differs specifically from the others. We know that in fact, very many factors influence the psychological make-up of any individual, so please consider the description of each Point as a general summary.

Where we needed to make a choice between precision (if that is possible in psychology!) and clarity, we favoured clarity. Please therefore read the descriptions below in a spirit of acceptance and compassion, asking how they might relate to you and the people around you.

It is also obvious that there are no good or bad types. There is only what we are and the Enneagram's only goal is to help us discover it.

In order to make reading the descriptions easier, we have used the expressions Ones and Twos to describe behaviours which we know are uniquely interpreted by each person who feels that this is their dominant psychological pattern. Please therefore take the expression One to mean people whose main filter is Point One and so on for each of the nine types.

POINT ONE

Predominantly a Perfectionist

I have many faults, but I do my best to avoid mistakes.
Anonymous

Habits and appearance

Ones are conscientious and tidy.

They like everything
to be in its place.

They are meticulous,
and work by the book.

They are afraid of making mistakes.

They have a high moral sense....

The ABC of the Enneagram

...for them, you're either right or wrong.

They are demanding,
but they avoid getting angry...

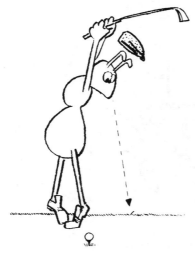

...even though imperfection annoys them...

...especially when others break the rules.

Understanding Ones

For Ones, life is about living to a code of human behaviour, a moral code. They value correctness highly and try to live in accordance with their principles. They are disappointed by the world's lack of respect for rules and beliefs.

Imperfection irritates them, and they are often seen as critical and demanding. They can always see how things can be improved, and find it hard to let things pass when they could be better. They also get annoyed when they notice that one of their close friends or family isn't trying their best.

They don't allow themselves to show emotion, so their anger is suppressed. In order to function, they need a just cause into which to channel their anger. Their internal conflict between rigidity and sensitivity causes tension (including muscular tension), which close friends and family can sometimes see.

You can count on them. When they are responsible for something, you can be sure that it will be done properly. For them work generally comes before pleasure, and they are able to put aside their own desires so that the work can get done, and done well.

They like:
- Behaving correctly
- Tidying up
- Being right
- Doing their job well
- Improving themselves

They dislike:
- Cheaters, those who break the rules
- Unfair criticism
- Disorder

The One personality

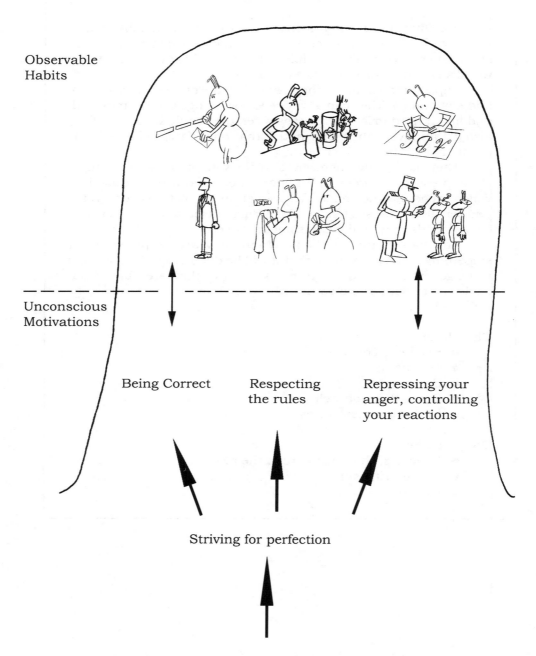

Observable
Habits

Unconscious
Motivations

Being Correct   Respecting
the rules

Repressing your
anger, controlling
your reactions

Striving for perfection

As a child, they believed: *The world punishes bad attitudes
and spontaneity.*

The ABC of the Enneagram

Perception of the world:

As children, Ones felt that the world condemns bad attitudes and impulses: *As soon as I let myself go, my spontaneity is punished and this hurts me.*

In order to compensate:

Ones chose to deserve love by being well behaved, by correcting their mistakes. They therefore developed a strong critical mind in order to prevent hurtful remarks from the outside: *It's when I strive toward perfection that I feel most worthy of being loved.* As a result of repressing their spontaneity, a strong internal anger developed.

Their system of values therefore developed around:

Law and order, rigour, love of work well done, integrity, discipline, effort, self-improvement.

Filters of perception were put in place:

Their attention is naturally focused on what is good or bad, respect for the rules, morals, correctness, and accuracy.

Their habitual defence mechanism:

Controlling their emotions and spontaneity, striving for perfection.

Under the influence of their passion

When they become annoyed with a perceived imperfection, Ones can ruin their lives with too much

Anger

When they allow themselves to be overwhelmed by their internal anger, Ones lose their balance, they move off-centre:

I see everything in the world through my judgmental filter.

Anger arises when they notice imperfection, whether it is their own, other people's or the world's in general:

If I fall into my trap of wanting everything to be perfect, anger makes me uncompromising, full of resentment. I lose all sense of humour and I become critical, unbending, inflexible and fussy.

The ABC of the Enneagram

When they control their passion

When they control their passion, Ones can accept things as they are: *I still see the imperfection of things, but what made me angry before is now a source of creativity. I can distance myself a little, channel the energy generated by anger and to put it to use for my other qualities.*

Ones can find

Serenity

Justice remains their principal value, but in a different way.

Serenity consists in getting past their preoccupation with perfection, accepting that neither the world nor themselves are perfect, overcoming their fear of doing the wrong thing ...

Instead of being perpetually angry, you can move to another level and accept the things that can't be changed, channel energy to changing what can be changed, and above all become capable of making the distinction between the two.

Anger

Curiously, although the passion of the One is called anger, the anger is most often not expressed. Ones control their anger:

It's not polite to lose your temper, it's not good; I always regret it when it happens.

Ones come across as very polite and well brought up people. They want to behave impeccably, to such an extent that they can be continuously resentful of others. They are therefore extremely critical and demanding, both of themselves and of others:

I can't understand people who don't go to any trouble to improve themselves.

Their efforts to be perfect sometimes lead to a rigid manner and a tendency toward the obsessive. A lot of Ones seem to fight against their desires, struggling between their two sides: the anxious adult who is accepted and the playful child who is denied. Anger and resentment are the result.

I can't stop myself from comparing reality with the way things should be. When I go into a room the first thing I see is the stain on the carpet. Even if it's minute, in the corner of the living room where no one can see it, it's the only thing I see. In a flash, I'm furious at this stain that has no business being there. Morally, it's the same story: I can't stop myself judging others' behaviour: 'this is good, this is bad.''

The anger has a moral basis: because they are full of good intentions, Ones want to reform the world, and tell others 'You ought to do this or that.'

I became my own policeman, a merciless critic in matters of discipline. I feel let down by people who don't follow the rules. For me, there's always a right way of doing things, which must be respected. I've always been a stickler for principles and when the children were late for a meal I made a big deal out of it. I think I was projecting my values onto them: do your best, always and everywhere.

When they are set in their type, this desire to change the world can go even further, to the point of wanting to reform anyone who isn't on the right path, almost like the Spanish Inquisition.

What Ones find difficult

Getting past my perfectionist values and finding my compassion or a sense of humour. Resentment, or even rage, can come over me in a flash when someone has cheated.

I can get obsessed with accuracy and meticulousness, *getting bogged down in the details. For example, when I'm tinkering with things, hanging a picture can take hours, because everything has to be absolutely perfect: the place, the height, etc, but I can't do it any other way; it would keep me awake at night if I did.*

Difficulties for others

Being judgmental. *My husband is representative of this type. It's difficult for me when he doesn't realise how angry he is, and that the way he speaks represses other people's views.*
When he feels criticised, his defensive reaction is to become judgmental. In that state of mind, he can't accept things as they are and he doesn't understand the fact that you don't share his point of view.

How you can encourage them

- Help them discover and accept their shadow of the naughty child.
- Help them understand that you can still love them even if they judge themselves to be imperfect.
- Point out to them the positive and successful aspects of the situation.
- Help them work on flexibility, letting go, smiling, and enjoyment.
- Help them learn to see perfection as something that evolves, not something fixed and final.

Advantages of being a One

I have a good instinct for recognising the morality *of a person or a plan. I can sort out what is fair and ethical, without getting entangled in emotion.*
I am prepared to sacrifice a lot for matters of principle. *Working hard and correctly is natural to me. I put integrity above everything. I have a pretty strict code of honour. I have to take action if I feel that a decision isn't morally right.*

Essential qualities

One personalities bring us these essential qualities:
- **Strictness**, sense of effort, the strength not to rest on one's laurels.
- **A sense of duty**: the will to follow the path that you know to be right.
- **Objective evaluation**, integrity, which will always take precedence over any thought of profit or prestige.
- **The desire to take action** to create a better world, trying hard to be the first to show a good example.
- The One energy is also our methodical side, honest and trustworthy: It's right to take whatever time is needed in order to do what I'm doing, well.

Famous personalities who show us Point One behaviour

Martin Luther, Pope John Paul II, Queen Elizabeth of England, Margaret Thatcher, Nelson Mandela, Mary Poppins, Hillary Clinton, Charlton Heston

How Ones can develop

Ones can blossom by agreeing to relax the rules, and allowing themselves to lose their temper, as well as:

Using the romantic energy of point Four:
- Identifying themselves with warm and friendly places where they can reveal a bit more of themselves.
- Analysing their emotions and sharing them
- Getting involved in theatre, singing, sports, decoration, framing pictures...in order to discover their artistic side, without judging it.

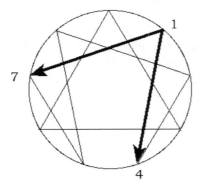

The ABC of the Enneagram

Using the epicurean energy of point Seven:
- Noticing when the internal critic appears... and smiling.
- Relearning how to enjoy themselves.
- Finding humour, mischievousness, the inner child
- Eliminating the word 'ought' from their vocabulary and doing whatever they like now and again.
- Recognising that others' mistakes might also be their right to be different.

POINT TWO

Predominantly Altruistic

What the point of being alive if not to take care of other people?
Anonymous

Habits and appearance

Twos are motivated by the
idea of being helpful.

The ABC of the Enneagram

They are tuned in to what other people need...

...are warm and considerate...

...like it when you need them

Relationships are more important
to them than anything else.

They love to comfort others...

...being of service....

...putting other people's
needs before their own...

...and being responsive to others' wishes.

Understanding Twos

Twos see themselves as the St. Bernard dog who comes to the rescue. They are very emotional, warm and considerate people.

They tune in to what others need, even if they don't know them well.

It's sometimes frustrating to be so aware of other's needs, especially their pain and unhappiness, because I can't help them as much as I would like to.

They like to take responsibility for others, and worry about what happens to them, even if their actions are most often guided by their need to be loved.

They can be clingy, protective, and maternal.

It's easy for me to give of my self. Sometimes I'd like to be able to say 'no' because in the end I put more energy into taking care of others than I do into taking care of myself. It hurts me when people think that I'm trying to manipulate or control them, when all I'm trying to do is to understand and help them.

They love to help, to be of service. They need others to need them. They sometimes feel like they're being used, even though it was they themselves who created an emotional dependence:

I give so that you'll love me.

Good relationships are essential to them, and they are ready to go to a lot of trouble in order to have them.

They like:
- Giving advice and encouragement
- Pleasing others, giving gifts
- Guessing what you need
- Being in the centre of a group

They dislike:
- Saying no
- Being alone
- Not being needed
- Having to wait
- Sitting alone in a corner

The Two personality

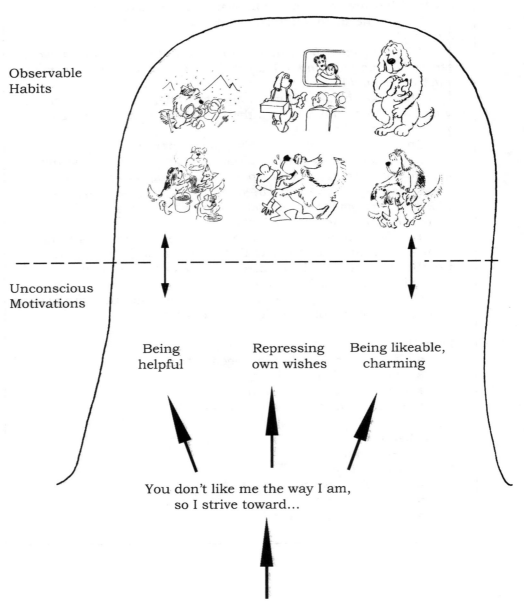

Observable
Habits

Unconscious
Motivations

Being
helpful

Repressing
own wishes

Being likeable,
charming

You don't like me the way I am,
so I strive toward...

As a child, they believed: *Everyone ignores me. I feel as
though I don't get enough love.*

The ABC of the Enneagram

Perception of the world:

As a child, Twos unconsciously believed that people don't love them for themselves, the way they are.

In order to adjust:

In order to satisfy their enormous emotional needs, Twos chose to win love through determination; by giving others what they are missing they hope of being loved in return. So they developed a finely-tuned sensitivity to what other people need, in order to be useful to them.

It's when I take care of others, when I help them, that I feel I'm alive.

Their value system therefore developed around:

Service, relationships and human warmth, feelings, and listening.

Perceptive filters were put in place:

Their attention is naturally focused on the needs of others:
Right now, who needs what and who needs me?

Their preoccupation is:

Adapting, forgetting themselves, and maintaining the St. Bernard image.

Their habitual defence mechanism:

Repressing and forgetting their own needs:
I don't know how to express what I want.

Under the influence of their passion

When they want to help at any cost, Twos ruin their lives with too much

Pride

When they let themselves be overwhelmed by the passion of being helpful, Twos lose their balance, and move off-centre by denying their own needs. They start being charming in order to please. Pride overtakes altruism.

Pride springs up when they notice that someone has a need. *Great, someone who needs help. I know how to help them.*

When Twos fall into their trap of wanting to be useful at any cost, they become manipulating: *By helping you, I create a connection, and you are going to have to pay attention to me.*

I anticipate others' needs to such a point, for example by offering them bread at the table, that I deprive them of their freedom to decide if they even want bread. By being considerate, I was influencing their choice.

When they control their passion

When they control their passion, Twos continue to see what others need, but they learn not to rush, and to stay humbly silent if the other person doesn't ask for help. Compassion still exists, but it is tempered by

Humility

Human warmth remains their principal value, but in a different way; Mother Theresa said:

I'm not fooling myself; I like to take care of others, but recognise I also get something out of it,

Twos are in the grip of Pride, when they are helpful while forgetting that they are doing it for themselves as well as for others. Humility involves, on the contrary, accepting your own nature. Once they realise this, Twos can admit that they are not needed, without feeling unloved.

They become themselves again when they no longer make choices depending on the needs of others, but on the basis of their own needs. By using the energy of pride to help them build their independence, they will find their freedom.

Pride

Pride is probably the best camouflaged passion. In our society, it's considered good to take care of others.

Thomas Condon (1994) describes pride thus:

Existing in order to give to others is a delicate matter, because you have to be very honest about your motivations and recognise that you have personal needs that can influence your desire to give.

Pride is when you see yourself as someone who doesn't need to receive: *When I was fit and healthy, I had plenty of outlets for my need to be generous. Even today (now I'm ill) it's still easier to give than to ask for what I want. Being helpful enables me to distance myself from the distress that lies behind my desire to please. It's like a spiral; the more you're proud of pleasing someone else, the more you suppress your own desires. You end up identifying completely with the needs of others.*

The driving force of this personality is the need to be loved. This enormous need for love gives rise to an inflated image of one's value and charm, to a need to attract attention, a need for privileges.

It goes without saying that people will remember my birthday; I would be distraught if someone forgot it. Pride sometimes pushes me not to remind anyone about the date, on purpose, in order to add intensity to my feelings.

In order to be able to help, Twos will charm in two ways: socially (taking care of others) or personally (erotically). This charm has several facets:

● Affection, warmth

For my friends, I'm an unconditional supporter. For others, I present myself as a possible confidant, like a shoulder to cry on which is at their disposal. I want to use all possible means to get the best for other people, even if it means being intrusive.

● Incredible abilities to adapt themselves in order to be what the other person wants.

I use my ability to sense what the other person wants in order to mould myself in that image. It's almost being an actor; I can play many roles depending on who I'm talking to.

It's just like the femme fatale, who can even go to the point of seducing someone, just to reassure themselves that they still have the capacity to be seductive.

What Twos find difficult

It's difficult for Twos to be alone; they feel useless when no one needs help:

> One day I realised that I was spending all my energy maintaining my image of the altruist instead of using it to develop my own potential. I realised that by taking care of others, I was trying to fill a feeling of emptiness. I remember once when I had some guests round to my house, after the last one left, I felt I was a gaping hole; I felt I no longer existed.

Difficulties for others

People around them start to feel uneasy when the Two's need to give becomes manipulating.

Their focus on health, feelings, and emotions can become tiresome for their circle of friends:

> I went to my grandmother's house to do some things for her, and on the way back, I spent some time chatting with the baker's wife; her daughter is sick and her son is unemployed. After leaving her, I took pity on a homeless man, and gave him a some money. His daughter was playing an accordion by his side ...

Twos can end up being helpful for the sake of being helpful, proud of the altruistic image that they want to present. Taking responsibility for others' needs can lead to a form of possessiveness (the Italian mother):

> One day a friend finally told me, 'You are too clingy, you've become too suffocating because you try too hard. You want so much to know what is best for me that I no longer feel free.'

How you can encourage them

- Give them positive feedback in situations where they aren't giving anything.
- Encourage them to speak on their own behalf, to express what they want.
- Avoid traps where they try to charm you by playing a role.
- Don't criticise them openly, but take time and be tactful.

Advantages of being a Two

● **It's a rare combination: tenderness combined with a fighting spirit**, always in the service of human relationships:
I've always been attracted by children or sick people. Because they need to be protected, there can be an exchange of love between us. They satisfy my thirst to give. I can also be proud of myself.
● **A gift for mind reading:**
I always know intuitively which gift will please someone the most.

Essential qualities

Twos can bring these qualities to the world:
● **Giving**. As all human beings are members of the same family, it's natural to give love to everyone: Give, give, give, there'll always be something left.
● **Intuition**. By listening to others, they've acquired this capacity to guess intuitively what they want.
● **Altruism**. The advice they give you in order to help you be more comfortable, is always kindly meant. They have a sense of what is good for you, on all levels; they can help you make your kitchen more functional as well suggest the exercise or diet that would do you the most good.
They remember your birthday and are truly concerned about your happiness. They can be a ray of human warmth. They dare to show you that you are valuable to them.

Famous personalities who show us Point Two behaviour

Mother Theresa, Princess Diana, Madonna, Audrey Hepburn, Jessica Lange, Harry Belafonte, Jerry Lewis.

The ABC of the Enneagram

How Twos can develop

Twos can blossom by coming to believe that they are as important as other people, and specifically by:

Using the boss energy of point Eight:
● Learning to say no.
● Discovering that they are more effective when they take their own needs into account.
● Expressing what they want.
● Not giving in order to be loved.
● Finding independent leisure activities where they depend on themselves.

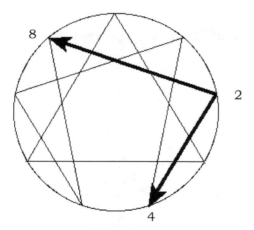

Using the romantic energy of point Four:
● Learning to take care of themselves.
● Analysing their emotions and sharing them.
● Participating in a decorative or artistic activity simply to please themselves, without having to charm or please others.

POINT THREE

Predominantly a Performer

Work is more pleasant than pleasure
Anonymous

Habits and appearance

Threes are competitors...

...winners, proud of their successes...

They have a talent for efficiency.

They know how to motivate others
and are intent on seeing the objectives reached.

They are good sales people.

They like to be able to measure
their progress...

...and cultivate business relationships.

Their appearance and the image
that they project are important...

...especially an image of success.

The ABC of the Enneagram

Understanding Threes

Threes have a happy and confident appearance, are energetic and effective. They seek out challenges and can end up being obsessed by performance.

I fought to succeed by exploiting and developing two roles: I was both a winner and an actor, able to change roles according to the situation.

They know how to change their image to fit in with other people's expectations:

I can easily change clothes three times if I go to three different parties in one evening.

They identify with what they do, because they think that everyone's value is based on their results and the prestige that follows. As achieving professional success occupies almost all of their time, they put aside any feelings or qualms in order to concentrate on objectives which will make them successful.

Because there's always something to do, Threes find it difficult to take the time to sit down and relax. They like to move fast and are upset when others don't make the most of the time they spend with them. Sometimes they want to take over a project that someone else is doing too slowly for their liking.

They like:
- Achieving and succeeding
- Being effective, busy, and active.
- Increasing their standard of living and prestige.
- Living for competition.

They dislike:
- Talking about feelings: It's a waste of time.
- Not having anything to do.
- Meetings that get bogged down or drag on.
- Failing, or missing a good opportunity.
- Having to wait.

The Three personality

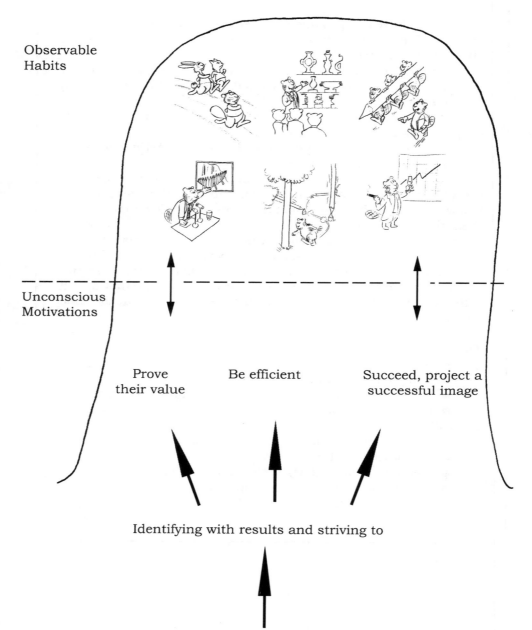

Observable
Habits

Unconscious
Motivations

Prove
their value

Be efficient

Succeed, project a
successful image

Identifying with results and striving to

As a child, they believed : *The world doesn't love me for
what I am, but for what I do.*

Perception of the world:

As children, Threes unconsciously believed that the world doesn't love them for what they are, but for what they do: *As a child, I had the impression that I was only loved for my good grades at school or my sports victories.*

In order to compensate:

Threes chose to win love through performance and action, and by projecting an image of success. *It's when I win, when I reach an objective, that I feel like I exist.*

Their system of values therefore developed around:
- Self-confidence
- Performance
- Prestige
- The image of success

Filters of perception were put in place:

Their attention is naturally focused on searching for approval:
I have students like this. They can project a different image to each of their teachers, depending on each one's personality.

Their preoccupation is:
- Searching for opportunities that are likely to lead to success.
- Adapting to other people's expectations.

Their habitual defence mechanism:

They identify with results; respect depends on social success and appearances, rather than on what one is in reality.

Under the influence of their passion

When they need to succeed at any cost, Threes ruin their
lives with too much

Deceit

When they allow themselves to be overwhelmed by the importance of
appearances, Threes lose their balance and move off-centre. They only
see the world through the filter of their need for success. As a result, they
lie to themselves and to others, massaging the truth, in order to project
the best possible image.

Their passion for the image they project, or for work, gives rise to
vanity:

*I can become hooked on work, not thinking about anything else. I never
seem to take any holidays, and I can't unwind.*

When they control their passion

When they control their passion, Threes can discover

Authenticity

Authenticity is an inner state where there's no longer a need to search for a role to identify with. Instead of looking to others in order to be what they expect, Threes in a state of authenticity can say: 'I am what I am and that's OK'. They no longer need to look to the outside and convince others that they are worthy of love: they know it deep inside themselves.

Authenticity is connected with hope:

Accepting that life will take care of what has to be done – without my efforts. Being able to let go and to accept that things get done through me rather than by me.

Threes who live in hope can turn their capacities of leadership, motivation, and achievement to the service of others, and experience the unconditional love that they have always been searching for.

The first step to take is to recognise that life can be happy in itself, without needing to produce, to manufacture things:

The most difficult thing was to discover that I exist independently of my actions.

Deceit[6]

Vanity lies in Threes' knowledge that they have the energy, the motivation, and the skills to succeed where others don't:.

I always believed everyone else was as ambitious as me; they just weren't so good at it. I still have a sneaking contempt for people who don't seem to want to succeed.

Deceit means believing that things won't get done unless you do them yourself, without considering that with time they can be done equally well and differently by others.

The passion of **deceit** does not mean Threes willfully deceive others. First and foremost they deceive themselves by identifying with the roles they have taken on. Since the need to be loved and accepted underpins the drive to succeed, Threes select arenas, both professional and social, which will gain the approval of the types of people they want to be accepted by.

They identify with their chosen roles, deceiving themselves that this is 'who they are,' and may not even notice if these identities change over time. Deceiving others is mainly a side-effect of this dynamic, coupled with Threes' ability to shift image. This is so subtle that they can be in a group of people and present themselves slightly differently to each person without it being noticed. For many Threes this is unconscious; others are aware they can do it, and see it as a useful skill.

Threes begin to be sceptical about their identification when they become aware that they will bend the truth to maintain the façade of success:

It may not be going great, but you say it is because you know it will be great... reality is relative to how I want it to be in the end. I miss so many cues because of this...you're fooling yourself, but you're fooling others too.

---

[6]This section is an extract from *Thorsons Principles of the Enneagram* by Karen Webb, Thorsons, London, 1996. Reproduced with author's permission.

The ABC of the Enneagram

What Threes find difficult

Facing your own truth:
I don't know what I'd find if I looked inside myself, but I'm sure it couldn't be good. So I prefer not to know, and I try very hard to avoid any form of self-examination. As a result, I live my life without reflection. Introspection will only depress me.

I've always liked to attract attention. *The best way is to have good results, but it's not the only way; you can also impress by appearances. I use all sorts of tricks to reinforce this image of success and prestige that I want to project; my makeup, my clothes, my car, my sex appeal. When I think about it today, proving my value, succeeding at any cost, was the only way of life that I knew.*

Difficulties for others

Being salesman of the month, making a deal, or networking was an obsession *for my husband for a very long time. He thought about nothing else, day and night. He could charm, play any role, and even invent sales pitches to achieve his ends. The children and I only existed after his job, if at all.*

Because he made results such a priority, *he no longer knew who he really was. He identified with and was lost in this role of 'look at me, I've got a big car.' He was capable of convincing others to support his objectives, sometimes against their values. Other people admired him, but I knew it was fake, that it wasn't him. It's taken him years to discover his true feelings.*

How you can encourage them

- Help them slow down their pace, to welcome and appreciate their feelings.
- Make them stop and smell the roses, listen to you.
- Tell them you love them the way they are.
- Let them know what's really important for you.

Advantages of being a Three

Thomas Condon (1994) says:

The basis of this character is the drive to succeed. All abilities are put to the service of performance and efficiency: precise thought, a rational and concrete mind, quickness of action, competitiveness, management ability, a combination of charm and a calculating mind, speaking ability... as if Threes were given all the advantages necessary to achieve the social success they dream of.

Essential Qualities

His confidence in himself is contagious. He gives you the impression that you can really do it. He has a gift for sales: emphasising the good points of a project, knowing what different steps to take, how to adapt to you; he also has this incredible overflowing energy. When I'm with him, I have the impression that he can't fail. He'll always find a solution, always convince or motivate someone to get us out of a tight situation.

At the beginning of our marriage, his only priority was his professional success. Later he discovered other values: family and friendship. He still expends an enormous amount of energy, but he spends more time with us.

Famous personalities who show us Point Three behaviour

John F. Kennedy, Tony Blair, Jacques Chirac, Jimmy Connors, Sharon Stone, Cindy Crawford, Brooke Shields, Walt Disney, Tom Cruise.

How Threes can develop

Threes can blossom by recognising their inner truth, and more precisely by:

Using the loyalist energy of point Six:
When Threes move to Six:
● They take off their mask, accept their weaknesses, and are able to notice of what's not working (in a couple for example).
● They accept their vulnerability and can give priority to other values besides activism or money.
● They become authentic and can show that they are more than the image they project.

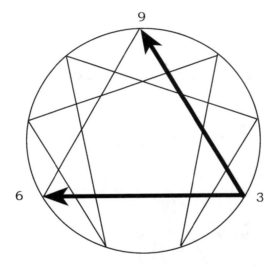

Using the mediating energy of point Nine:
● Slowing down the pace will enable Threes to detach themselves from performance, to listen to their feelings and physical sensations (fatigue for example).
● In Nine, Threes can put failure into perspective and are able to ask themselves what really matters to them.

POINT FOUR

Predominantly a Romantic

Nothing makes us so great as a great sorrow.
Alfred de Musset

Habits and appearance

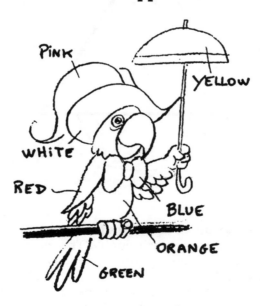

Fours are unique individuals, focused on beauty and aesthetics.

They are emotionally sensitive...

...to the point of seeking out
intensity and drama.

They are hypersensitive to criticism...

...with a definite theatrical side.

At times, they envy what others have.

They feel different, apart from everyone else.

They sometimes have the feeling
of being abandoned and are prone to depression.

They also have a nostalgic and melancholy
streak, directed towards the past.

The ABC of the Enneagram

Understanding Fours

Fours are great romantics who have strong, intense emotions. They are attracted by beauty, uniqueness, and what is different. They prefer nostalgia and melancholy to banality.

The importance they place on emotions gives them enormous creativity. They are sensitive and have a need to express their emotions; think of Rimbaud, Baudelaire, Leonard Cohen, or Piaf. Because of the depth of their emotions, they feel different from others.

They need warmth: for someone to listen to them, for someone to take the time to share their feelings and intensity of life. They are idealists looking for a meaning to existence. They are often at ease and effective in the important moments of life, both theirs and yours.

They like:
- Sharing their feelings.
- Using their creativity: in the way they dress, in the way they work, in the decoration of a dish or a room...
- Experiencing unique moments, intense and exceptional.

They dislike:
- Banality, routine, the everyday.
- Criticism, lack of respect.
- Having to follow a procedure to the letter.

The Four personality

Observable
habits

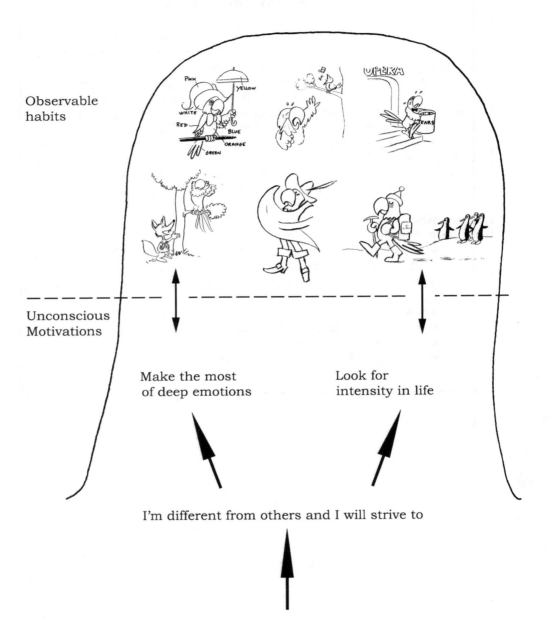

Unconscious
Motivations

Make the most
of deep emotions

Look for
intensity in life

I'm different from others and I will strive to

As a child, they believed: *I was abandoned.*

The ABC of the Enneagram

Perception of the world:

As children, Fours unconsciously felt they were abandoned. It was as if there was a big void; something important was missing. This feeling of abandonment characterises their life.

In order to compensate:

They imagined that they could fill this feeling of something missing by looking for the abundance that existed before the abandonment.

Their value system therefore developed around:
- Expressing their feelings.
- Being understood despite being different: creativity, romanticism, and sense of aesthetics.
- Finding a meaning in life: the importance of symbols.

Filters of perception were put in place:

Their attention is naturally focused on:
- What's missing or what's not available: object, love, work...
- Beauty in what is far away, past, or yet to come.
- The inadequacy of what they have.
- Intensity of feelings: a good depression is better than suffering the banality of everyday life.

Their preoccupation is:
- Making the most of their emotions, feelings.
- Only looking for what is unique, intense, or elitist.
- Avoiding the gloom of the present and escaping from the dreariness of the ordinary.

Their habitual defence mechanism:

They idealise what isn't available; their imagination will, for example, magnify the value of the scarf they don't have (although they have plenty of others). Consequently, emotions and feelings become more important than real facts.

Under the influence of their passion

When they allow the feeling of abandonment to dominate, Fours
ruin their lives with too much

Envy

When they allow themselves to be overwhelmed by envy, they lose
their balance and move off centre. They see everything in the world through
their emotional filter.

Envy arises from their inability to be satisfied with things as they
are. Because they are afraid of finding the present too mediocre, they
fabricate emotional intensity in order to spice up the ordinary. They prefer
situations that provoke anxiety or ecstasy to dreary everyday life.

As a result, they spend their time dreaming about whatever ideal is
unattainable. It must be unattainable because attaining it would appease
their emotions, and if they no longer had emotions, they would feel they
no longer existed.

They confuse emotional intensity with authenticity; they reject the
truth when it is too banal, they get depressed when the truth doesn't
meet their need for intensity.

When they control their passion

Fours continue to tingle with emotion, but they've learned how to
manage their ups and downs. They are in a state of

Equanimity

Equanimity, or evenness of temper, is about feeling in harmony with
yourself, whatever the circumstances may be. Envy, on the other hand, is
(always)always focused on something outside you. When Fours find
equanimity, they realise that they already have all they need and that
they are perfectly fine the way they are. They know how to keep their
balance without having to prove their value by searching for intensity.

Envy[7]

Envy is not jealousy, but a constant sensation in the heart of something missing, and a yearning to fill the emptiness. Fours seek completion, but it feels like trying to attain the unattainable: disappointment is an overriding issue most of the time.

Their attention focuses on what is missing, so what is present is not good enough, thus confirming that something must be lacking. Fours look around them and feel that if only they could have that particular thing, they would be all right. It could range from envying someone an unusual item of clothing, a character trait, or nurturing parents, to beautiful surroundings, or imagining everyone else has the perfect relationship they can never have for themselves.

Envy also fuels the highly individual elitism of the Four. Envying others, they do not seek to be like them but to express the unique and real in themselves:

> There was always the idealised image – in college I wrote a poem about all the girls I'd gone out with, and there was always something wrong. I approached people and experiences with an idealised image rather than allowing the experience to be what it was. I had an idea of how I wanted it to be, and then the experience had to measure up. That's been characteristic of a lot of things I've done.

Melancholy[8]

Melancholy is a mental focus which gives life a bitter-sweet flavour. Life is not about anything as trivial as happiness: when Fours experience joy it is passionate and deep, but includes the knowledge that the opposite is never far away. They recognise and embrace the idea that true creativity and perfect love must be suffered for, in fact are born from suffering:

> I often feel misunderstood and alone because I feel different from others. Sometimes my sensitivity is criticised, to the point of claiming that I'm overdoing it. In fact, inside I'm always looking for an emotional relationship that's at the same time deep and emotionally strong.

Fours welcome deeply-felt emotion as a source of creative energy. There is a clear dividing line for them between melancholy, which is a true and meaningful emotion, and depression which may feel real at the time but is the result of being stuck in a negative loop.

> That's the difference between depression and melancholy: melancholy is part of the creative urge; depression destroys it.

---

[7] This section is an extract from *Thorsons Principles of the Enneagram* by Karen Webb, Thorsons, London, 1996. Reproduced with author's permission.
[8] Ibid

The ABC of the Enneagram

Difficulties for others

When he embarks on his tragic-romantic spiral, it gets crazy: his voice trembles, he launches tirades worthy of a tragic actor. I can't decide whether to applaud the performance or confront this manic habit of magnifying emotion to the point of hurting himself and suffering. When he has calmed down and I talk to him, he tells me that he needs it, that it's what drives him.

How you can encourage them

- Don't get sucked into their game; be a stable reference point.
- Emphasise what they can have, here and now.
- Help them use their enormous creative energy to get themselves back in balance: singing, dancing, or any other form of artistic activity will help them channel this energy, to tame it, and little by little, they will learn to master their bouts of melancholy.

Advantages of being a Four

Some people say that I have a flair for drama. It's true that whenever there's a marriage or a funeral in the family, I feel like I'm in my element. It's the type of intense situation that's extraordinary for others but is part of my everyday life... in my imagination. So I know how to manage the situation better than other people: who to invite, how to arrange the decorations ... Whenever it's a question of reasoning with your emotions, I'm in my element.

Most people find me excessive. But you don't know how good it feels to let yourself be carried by a wave of emotion. I cry regularly at the theatre or at the movies, but these tears have such a satisfaction, such spice...Deep inside I live for the hope of finding these moments.

Essential Qualities

- **Fours are fervent admirers of beauty**. They tend to know how to find meaning in life; they are experts in metaphor.
- **They put us in contact with the symbolic side of things**. They know how to help us get in touch with the value of forms, colours, and movement. They help us to experience our emotions in the present, rather than avoiding them. They show us how to express feelings; they take the time to internalise them and express what they're feeling.
- **Fours attach value to the aesthetics of beauty** and to the tragic nature of existence. In some ways, people of this type can transform the suffering of life into something meaningful.
- **As friends they have exceptional empathy**, understanding the dilemmas and suffering of close friends or family members.

Famous personalities who show us Point Four behaviour

The nostalgic poetry of Keats or Shelley, of Baudelaire or Lamartine...
Prince Charles of England, Vincent Van Gogh, Marguerite Duras, Rudolf Nureyev, Edith Piaf, Marlon Brando, Virginia Woolf, Thomas Merton...

How Fours can develop

Fours can blossom by lessening their dependence on strong emotions, and more precisely by:

Using the perfectionist energy of point One:
Fours can balance out their passionate side by adding some objectivity and rigour to their lives. In this way, they will discover a reality independent of their emotional life. They will be able to use common sense to balance their creative imagination.

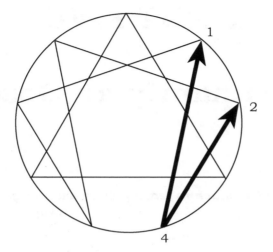

Using the altruist energy of point Two:
By moving to Two, Fours can:
● Leave behind their individualism and discover their capacity to give.
● Develop their listening skills and start being interested in the feelings and emotions of others as well as in their own.

POINT FIVE

Predominantly an Observer

There is so much to learn just by watching.
Anonymous

Habits and appearance

Fives are observers, loners concerned to preserve their personal space.

They are logical and analytical...

...like to understand,
have the big picture...

...they tend to observe rather than participate.

Being with others for a long time tires them.

The ABC of the Enneagram

They are independent...

... and self-sufficient.

They prefer thought to action...

...and have trouble expressing their emotions.

The ABC of the Enneagram

Understanding Fives

Fives are loners, entrenched in their inner world like a hermit in his ivory tower. They prefer thought to action.

They are calm and analytical, not really fond of social contacts, and sometimes appear cold and distant. They have a talent for synthesising ideas.

Fives need more solitude than most people. They generally prefer to watch what happens rather than participate in it. They don't like talking about themselves or their feelings. They are more successful at getting in touch with their emotions when they are alone. They are never bored being alone because their mind is always active. They feel the need to protect their time and their energy. Often they prefer to lead a simple life, without complications, and as independent as possible.

They like:
- Living in privacy, discretion, even silence.
- Observing, stepping back.
- Knowing, understanding.
- Thinking, finding out why things are the way they are.

They dislike:
- Intrusion into their personal space.
- Things that are worldly, unnecessary or superfluous.
- Noise.
- Trivial conversations.
- Questions about their emotions.
- The unexpected.
- Emotional displays.
- On the spot decision making.

The Five personality

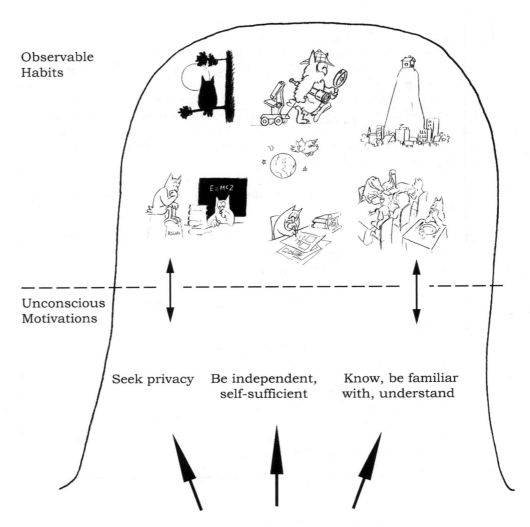

Observable
Habits

- -

Unconscious
Motivations

Seek privacy   Be independent,   Know, be familiar
self-sufficient   with, understand

I have to protect my privacy and I will strive to

As a child, they believed : *The world is intrusive.*

Perception of the world:

As children, Fives unconsciously believed the world was invasive and intrusive.

In order to compensate:

Fives chose to protect themselves from external intrusion. They protected themselves by putting distance between themselves and others and by acquiring information: *If I understand the situation completely, I won't ever be taken by surprise.*

Their system of values therefore developed around:

Thinking, knowing, being familiar with, understanding, and protecting personal space.

Filters of perception were put in place:

Their attention is naturally focused on:
- Observing and conceptualising things.
- Controlling their feelings.
- Accepting things as they are.
- Separating and segmenting things and time.

Their preoccupation is:
- Seeking privacy: they are stingy with their time and presence.
- Limiting their needs: being self-sufficient is reassuring.
- Managing their emotions (especially fear), protecting themselves against intrusions.
- Foreseeing things, anticipating demands.
- Not wasting energy.

Their habitual defence mechanism:

They tend to isolate themselves, to entrench themselves in their inner world.

Under the influence of their passion

When they are afraid of being invaded, Fives ruin their
lives by too much

Avarice

Avarice comes from fear of not having enough. To counteract this,
Fives become hoarders, particularly protecting their time, their presence,
their personal space... They entrench themselves in the intellectual world.
*When I go into my spiral of wanting to know everything, I can become
cold, distant, intellectually arrogant...*

When they control their passion

When they control their passion, Fives continue to need personal space,
but they accept that they need to live in the world.
They are in a state of

Non-attachment

*Before I understood, I used complete detachment as a way of calming
my fear. I tried to recreate the feeling of having enough by swallowing
all the information that I could get my hands on: newspapers, books...
Since this wasn't enough to reassure me, I tried to consume as little as
possible.*

*When I managed to tame my fear of not having enough, I began to be
able to come closer to other people. To my surprise, I discovered that
human contact, far from depriving me of energy, actually gives me
something. I still keep a certain distance, a non-attachment, but I have
become less stingy with my presence.*

Avarice[9]

The energy capacity of Fives is sapped by avarice.

Avarice is an emotional preoccupation, in which Fives feel they are always potentially lacking the means for safe survival, and they are avaricious of whatever enables them to feel secure and independent. This is not usually anything material, as they minimise physical needs, but information which enriches their inner world and helps them feel prepared for the onslaughts of the outer world:

If I were to be shipwrecked, or if some kind of disaster happened, I know I'd survive where other people wouldn't. For one thing I can get by on very little, in fact I enjoy not having too much – otherwise I feel weighed down and trapped – but also, I've read all the survival manuals. Specially nowadays it seems to make sense...

They also feel an intense need – a sort of greed – for private space and time, both for safety's sake and for nourishment:

Independence is a preoccupation – something I value a lot. The inner world is self-sustaining, I could live by myself and survive. Privacy is actually nourishing. I love being alone with no demands on me at all – it's ecstasy.

What Fives find difficult

Sharing information:

Although most Fives know a lot about a lot of things, when you ask them something (which usually seems to them like a demand), they will reply calmly, but will give as little information as possible, so as to discourage the other person from prolonging the conversation. There is no malice intended; the less they give, the more they feel secure.

So, for example, in meetings, if the agenda isn't clear, they instinctively withdraw; they worry that their finite supply of energy will be sapped. Unexpected demands frighten them, because for them the unknown is generally uncomfortable:

There's a risk that I'd be dragged into something which I'm not prepared for... There's a real feeling of danger, even in minor circumstances like suddenly being invited to a party. First I need to consider how available I can be, what others might want from me, and what I can give.

My inner life is rich, but I can't easily express it. The thing I dread most is to talk to someone wants to know about my emotions.

Moving from thought to action:

I like designing projects. But when the design is ready, I prefer to hand it over to others, who will put it into action.

---

[9] This section is an extract from *Thorsons Principles of the Enneagram* by Karen Webb, Thorsons, London, 1996. Reproduced with author's permission.

The ABC of the Enneagram

Difficulties for others

Some days, you can't even talk to him. He's lost in thought, and doesn't want to talk.
When he goes inside his safety zone, he seems cold and distant to me. I feel as though he's in his fortress, surrounded by walls, and that no emotion can reach him.

How you can encourage them

● Help them discover the pleasures of life.
● Help them talk about themselves.
● Don't bombard them with your feelings.
● Respect their independence and their secret gardens.
● Be clear about what you want, especially when you're ask them to do something.

Advantages of being a Five

Non-attachment has something magical to it: it's as though you can be part of the game of life without being sucked in by it. It's a great gift to be able to distance yourself from the situation, so that you can think about it without getting too personally involved. Once this ability saved my life. While we were mountain climbing, our roped party fell, and thanks to my emotional distance, I was able to think calmly, even though there was blood everywhere and everything happened very quickly...

Essential Qualities

● Fives show us how to live in the external world while keeping internal balance by being calm and lucid.
● They show us the advantage of stepping back, of detaching ourselves from our emotions when faced with events.
● They remind us about forgotten qualities like discretion, non-verbal language, modesty and objectivity.
● Through their conceptualising ability, Fives often have a sixth spatial sense, which we often see in architects and engineers.

They remind us that sensitivity and human warmth can be expressed in ways other than through emotional display.

Famous personalities who show us Point Five behaviour

The classic analogy is that of the hermit, the image of a solitary man wearing a long coat, walking alone down a path. It is an ancient image, symbolising man's ability to isolate himself from his emotions and the external world in order to get in touch with his inner life.

Krishnamurti, The Buddha, Albert Einstein, Madeline Stowe, Stefan Edberg, Jeremy Irons, J.D. Salinger, Emily Dickinson.

How Fives can develop

Fives can blossom by putting aside their solitude, and trusting more, and particularly by:

Using the epicure energy of point Seven:
● Noticing associations of ideas and their creative imagination (Newton and the apple).
● Experimenting with adventure, taking risks, turning thoughts into action.
● Trying out curiosity, humour, enthusiasm,
● Indulging in pleasure, which will enable them to get closer to the world in ways which are not intellectual.

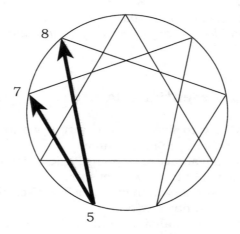

The ABC of the Enneagram

Using the boss energy of point Eight:
- Trying out a positive kind of aggressiveness.
- Using conviction in order to make things happen.
- Taking the courage to express themselves more often.
- Gathering the energy to go forward. The Five energy is often compared to an ebb tide: it's strong but retiring. The Eight energy can bring the flood tide.

POINT SIX

Predominantly a Loyalist

To doubt is to recognise the possibility of hope.
Lautreamont

Habits and appearance

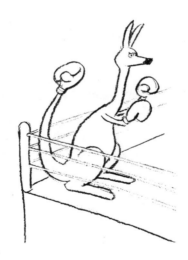

Sixes are careful types; they are
motivated by the need for security.

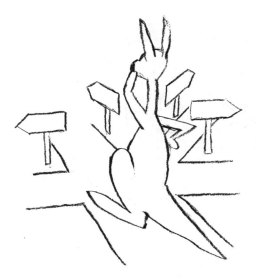

They are often prey to doubt...

...they tend to worry about possible disappointments...

...they imagine the worst possible scenario...

...and prefer things to be predictable

The ABC of the Enneagram

They overestimate danger...

...and tend to ask for advice.

They don't trust others easily...

...but once they give their trust,
they have a strong sense of loyalty.

The ABC of the Enneagram

Understanding Sixes

Sixes have lots of imagination, and often use it for predicting what could threaten their security:

I'm always imagining the worst: what if something breaks down..., if it rains..., and if I arrive late...

They have a talent for detecting flaws and what is left unsaid in arguments.

When faced with danger, they are torn between two extreme behaviours: fight or flight. Sixes would like to be more trusting, but instead they tend to be suspicious of people and things. Their relationship to authority is ambivalent; on the one hand it gives them security, but on the other, they don't trust it.

Doubt is often present, which makes them often speak in reaction to what you say, rather than stating their own opinion. Once they are committed to a person or cause, they are unfailingly loyal.

They have a tendency to identify with the underdog.

They like:
- Clear-cut situations.
- The feeling of security.
- Loyalty.
- Having enough time to prepare, to adapt.
- Playing devil's advocate to test your sincerity.

They dislike:
- Vague or unpredictable authority figures.
- Treason, deceit.
- Ambiguous situations.
- The unexpected.
- Smooth talkers, superficial arguments.
- Starting something without knowing where it's going.
- Someone trying to pull the wool over their eyes.

The Six personality

Observable
Habits

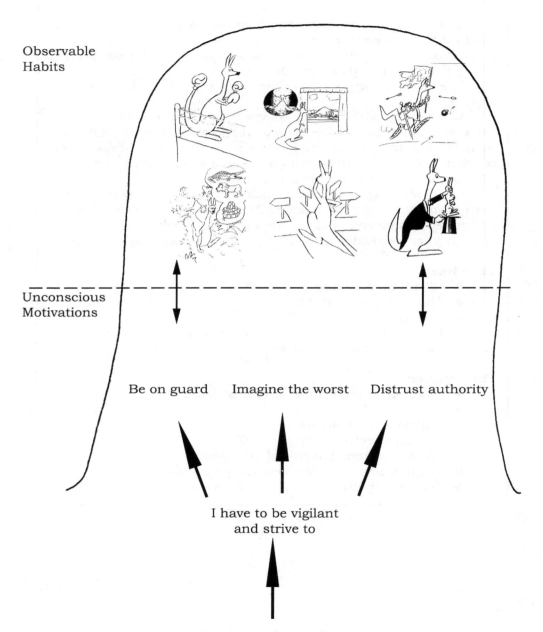

Unconscious
Motivations

Be on guard   Imagine the worst   Distrust authority

I have to be vigilant
and strive to

As a child, they believed: *I was betrayed:
the world is threatening and unstable.*

The ABC of the Enneagram

Perception of the world:

As children, Sixes unconsciously perceived that the world was not reliable: *I was betrayed.* Their base camp isn't a safe place and will never be.

In order to compensate:

Sixes chose to ensure their security through vigilance:
Sometimes, I see myself as a sentry on guard, faced with a possible attack. My life revolves around fear, I bounce between submission and defiance, always reacting against potential danger or a hidden agenda.

Their system of values therefore developed around:

Reliability, loyalty, imagination, sensitivity, and intuition.

Filters of perception were put in place:

Their attention is naturally focused on:
● Being on the lookout for possible danger (often magnified).
● Looking for technicalities and ambiguities.
● The relationship with authority.
● Identification with the weak and oppressed.

Their preoccupation is:

● Imagining the future consequences of a decision. Imagining the worst possible scenario sometimes prevents them from acting.
● Protecting themselves against all forms of danger.
● Distrusting success, which for them is synonymous with pretentious display.
● Questioning people about their motivations, in order to eliminate doubt.

Their habitual defence mechanism:

Projection: they project their fears onto the future and their doubt on to the person they're speaking to.

Under the influence of their passion

When they are full of doubt, Sixes ruin their lives with too much

Fear

Sixes then become either paralysed by doubt, or hyper-aggressive towards authority, rushing towards danger.

When they go into their spiral of wanting to protect themselves against any risk, their natural suspicion and their need for clarity become excessive. Their doubt sometimes takes them to the point of questioning their own common sense.

When I'm desperate to know if the world is trustworthy, a negative piece of information can cancel out years of positive signals. When my mind is stuck in fear, it generates projections of incredible strength and credibility. Then it's difficult to accept that I'm 'inventing worst case scenarios for myself' and that I'm looking for a sign to corroborate the feeling of threat that is actually of my own making, because of my pattern of thinking.

The ABC of the Enneagram

When they control their passion

Doubt is still present, but Sixes are able to transform it into

Courage

Courage and faith

Courage is to have enough trust in your intuition to rely on it:

It sometimes happens, in the middle of terrifying danger, that I simply know what I have to do and actually do it. In these cases, it seems to me that I give real life permission to speak to me (instead of my projections), and enable me act correctly.

In practical terms, the best way to stop the projections is to get in touch with the body, to use the energy of fear in some other way which is not mental activity.

Faith, by definition, can't be based on proof. It's an act of trust, which goes beyond fear:

Through a conscious act of giving my trust, I can put myself in a state where I can tackle any situation without automatically questioning its genuineness or looking for a hidden catch.

Fear[10]

Doubt, rather than overt fear is what defines Sixes. It is natural to feel doubtful of the trustworthiness of anything when there is a constant feeling of imminent threat. Doubt also masks fear by allowing Sixes to feel that, since everything is doubtful, the probability of negative outcomes is real.

Sixes are hyper-vigilant, scanning for sources of possible threat. Their senses are acute, even able to tune into separate conversations in a crowded room. Mentally, they question situations, what others say, and their own thoughts, and they focus on the future, imagining worst possible scenarios in an attempt to feel safe.

Alertness and an adrenaline high are part of fear. Sixes often say they enjoy their habitual state and do not want to lose the fear because they would lose the energy.

The two classic responses to fear – fight or flight – result in two types of Sixes. Some use both responses, depending on circumstances, but many lean to one or the other.

Counter-phobic Sixes pre-empt fear by confronting danger and going toward it:

I get my retaliation in first.

These people, men or women, can be aggressive, independent, and seem afraid of nothing. Their snarl, however, is that of a creature at bay, not a predator:

A Kiwi man has to be macho – sports, drinking, fighting – I was in there with all the rest; more so. I just couldn't have ponced around going 'I'm scared'. Actually I'm terrified most of the time, though I only realised it recently.

Phobic Sixes prefer 'flight.' They are usually aware of their fear and avoid potentially harmful situations, Unassertive, even timid, it is phobic Sixes who are most likely to consciously avoid success as it gives a high profile and is therefore dangerous:

I found myself in a niche – literally, in a corner – and sat there and got on with things, even when I disagreed with how I was being asked to do them.

They are also the most likely to seek out and follow an authority whom they judge to be trustworthy, with the danger that in their search for safety they may project 'good' qualities on to unworthy leaders.

---

[10] This section is an extract from *Thorsons Principles of the Enneagram* by Karen Webb, Thorsons, London, 1996. Reproduced with author's permission.

The ABC of the Enneagram

Cowardice is a facet of the imagination, rather than unwillingness to face things. The mental focus of anticipating a negative outcome was expressed by William Shakespeare as: 'Cowards die many times before their deaths...' (Julius Caesar), and Sixes confront the day-to-day equivalents of death almost constantly in their minds.

Their behaviour is rarely 'cowardly,' but this mental focus underlies procrastination, projection of imagined feelings on to others, intense curiosity and the need to remain unaffected and in control of their environment.

Sixes run over issues again and again, even when they have already got an answer to their question.. Often excellent conversationalists (which is also a way of staying in control of situations) they easily take up the devil's advocate role. They like to qualify and explore the doubtful edges of things, and may take an opposing stance just for fun, as well as to clarify things:

You pointed out yesterday that I say' but' a lot. Well, yes... but isn't that just because I want to find out the answers?

What Sixes find difficult

Relationships with authority:

Authority was a problem for a long time. In school, I was always in a bizarre relationship with my teachers, somewhere between distrust and rebellion.

Imagination:

Mallebranche (1994) once said:

Imagination is the mad woman in the house. Reining in my imagination when it gets carried away, is as difficult as breaking a wild horse. It goes off in all directions and I have to ground myself in practical things in order to prevent the imaginary from becoming more important than reality.

Doubt:

I don't know anything worse than doubt. It pushes itself in everywhere, elbowing everything out of its way, whether it's justified or not. It's really poisonous; it interferes with my thoughts, with my actions, to the point where it makes me hesitate when I'm faced with things that seem obvious during the day when the fog lifts, when my ideas are clearer.

Difficulties for others

Some days it's discouraging. She verbally attacks me while making me the target of all her fears. Her doubts become certainties. It's not playing devil's advocate, it's paranoia!

My son plays in tennis tournaments. The day before, he's shaking with anxiety, he magnifies the qualities of his opponent and minimises his own potential. When you listen to him, he's a Lilliputian and his opponent is Gulliver or Goliath. When he comes out on the court, sometimes he plays terribly because of his lack of confidence, and on other days he masters his fear and plays like a champion. When I see what he's like, I wonder whether Henri Leconte wasn't like that.

How you can encourage them

- Take the time to listen to them.
- Be attentive and calm; you should reassure them, give them confidence.
- Draw their attention to what is working well at the moment.
- Comment on their successes.
- Give them optimistic alternatives to their fears; show your faith in the future.
- Be reliable and clear in your relationship with them.

Advantages of being a Six

Being used to danger:
When there's a crisis, my habit of mobilising all my forces to face danger becomes an asset.

Intuition:
After years of strict vigilance, my sixth sense has become my most important quality. Once I learned how to master my projections, I was able to develop my intuitive sense to the point where some of my friends say I'm a medium.

Quick wittedness:
I have a flair for repartee, because often I anticipate what people will say.

Essential Qualities

This combination of fear and courage generates faith. One without the other is just madness; courage without fear becomes foolhardiness, and fear without courage becomes powerlessness.

Lacordaire said: 'All I can know about tomorrow is that Providence will rise before the sun'. Sixes show us this certainty, which lies beyond fear and proof. Because they have crossed the desert of doubt, Sixes have become the champions of trust. They also show us the importance of searching for truth beyond appearances.

The ABC of the Enneagram

In their relations with others, they have a talent for establishing and maintaining clear and reliable relationships.

Famous personalities who show us Point Six behaviour

Joan of Arc, Michelangelo, John MacEnroe, Paul Newman, Robert Redford, Woody Allen, Julia Roberts.

How Sixes can develop

Sixes can blossom by trusting others, by being more in their body and less in their heads, and more precisely by:

Using the performer energy of point Three:
- Self-confidence, the capacity to put themselves forward, to sell themselves, to dare to take centre-stage.
- The ability to make firm decisions, without being tempted to go back on them.

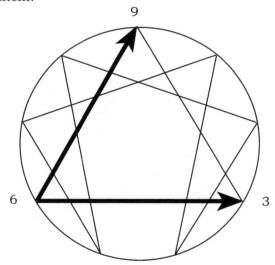

Using the mediator energy of point Nine:
- A slower pace will enable them to put the possible dangers they see into perspective.
- Paying attention to their physical sensations will calm their spirit, enabling them put things in perspective and reconnect with nature.
- The ability to focus on themselves, instead of constantly reacting to the outside.
- The ability to relate to others without making assumptions.

POINT SEVEN

Predominantly an Epicure

You only live once, make the most of it!
Anonymous

Habits and Appearance

Sevens are always on the lookout for pleasure.

They can't stand being closed in.

They have trouble finishing what they start.

They are enthusiastic and optimistic...

...they tend to get carried away by whatever is new.

The ABC of the Enneagram

They like having lots of plans...

They are always on the move...

...They have a tendency to underestimate danger.

Even in difficult situations, they tend to be positive.

The ABC of the Enneagram

Understanding Sevens

Sevens are quick to talk and like to play. They tend not to feel tied to any commitment that is imposed on them by others. Always on the go, they like to plan and have the choice between several possibilities; commitment is a trap.

Sevens are optimists. They like to take on new projects. Cheerful and lively, their life is a party; champagne flows in their veins. Life is without limits, full of wide open spaces and adventure.

Their quick mind jumps rapidly from one idea to another, which enables them to make connections between lots of ideas. They like doing lots of things at once, such as reading several books at a time. They start a lot of things but rarely see them through. They have trouble concentrating on difficult and repetitive tasks. They like to have an overall view of the way things fit together, but once they understand it, they tend to get bored. They have trouble facing the uncomfortable side of life, and prefer to turn their thoughts to more pleasant ideas.

They like:
- Variety.
- Adventure, travel.
- A good laugh.
- Being charming.
- Making plans.
- Collecting pleasures.

They dislike:
- Feeling shut in.
- Taking great pains over details.
- Doing the same thing for a long time.
- Boredom.
- Routine.
- Meetings that go on and on.
- Days when nothing happens.

The Seven personality

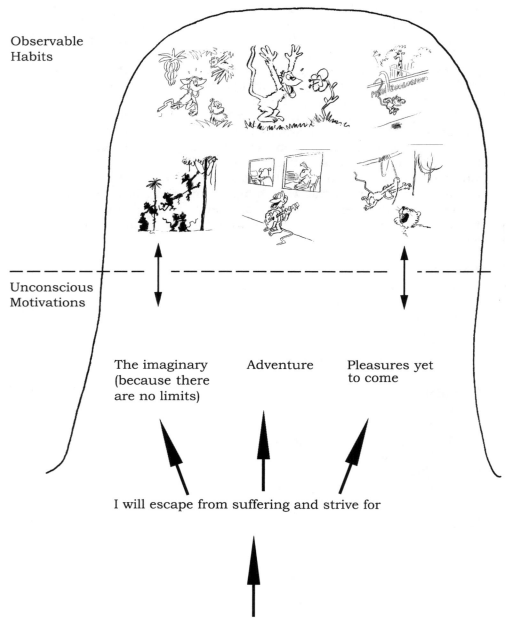

Observable
Habits

Unconscious
Motivations

The imaginary
(because there
are no limits)

Adventure

Pleasures yet
to come

I will escape from suffering and strive for

As a child, they believed: *I suffer because of the limits
this restrictive world imposes on me.*

The ABC of the Enneagram

Perception of the world:

As children, Sevens unconsciously perceived the world as frustrating and restrictive:

I like my freedom and I suffer if I am limited to a single choice.

In order to compensate:

Sevens chose to avoid suffering by escaping into their imagination, towards future adventures and pleasures.

Their system of values therefore developed around:

Making the most of being alive, getting as much pleasure as possible, seeking out variety, concentrating exclusively on the bright side of things.

Filters of perception were put in place:

Their attention is naturally focused on:
- Having lots of projects on the go at the same time.
- Making lots of plans in order to keep lots of options open.
- Having fun.
- Collecting information.

Their preoccupation is:

- Looking for excitement and novelty.
- Only seeing the positive, even in difficult situations.
- Being charming, either to get you on their side, or just for fun.

Their habitual defence mechanism:

- Rationalising and intellectualising.
- Keeping things superficial, running away from boredom, obstacles and difficulties.

Under the influence of their passion

When they are afraid of being shut in, Sevens ruin their lives with too much

Gluttony

Nothing satisfies them; they always need more. Because they're afraid of missing something, they become gluttons; they can't stop eating, laughing, moving on to more pleasures....

When they go into a spiral of wanting everything immediately, they can't focus; they can't make the most of the present and become eternally dissatisfied.

The ABC of the Enneagram

When they control their passion

When they control their passion, Sevens still need pleasure
and diversity, but they can channel their energy and show

Sobriety

    Sobriety is a state in which emotions are centred and mastered. At
first, Sevens seek fulfilment by trying to experience everything. When they
start to work with their type, they realise that true pleasure comes from
long-term commitment and involvement. They become more realistic.

    This acceptance that life is sometimes painful enables them to
experience joy on a deeper level.

Gluttony[11]

The energy capacity of Sevens is eaten away by gluttony, otherwise called greed. **Gluttony** is the emotional habit that keeps fear at bay by focusing on the myriad enjoyable possibilities.

Sevens do not pick one good thing and experience it in all its depth, but sample a little of all the best available:

It's in everything I do, the most mundane. For example, I like lots of textures and different flavours in my food. New projects – ah, the potential – this one will be the one – until it takes too much effort and the next one comes along. My ultimate goal is to experience everything.

Often gluttony masks anxiety about deep-felt emotion. Sevens want to move on, get out of the situation, and not feel it:

When something bad happens to me I immediately find a whole lot of ways to divert my attention and get busy and get out of it. Non-action or hanging around wallowing in emotion is, if I'm truthful, frightening, though what I think is: 'What's the point, we've felt it, let's get on with life now'.

Moving from one experience to another, and living in the mind where there are no limits to what can be experienced, can make Sevens, for all their charm, inaccessible:

I'm not present most of the time – I'm off in the future, and it's very pleasant there. Why should I come back?

Planning as a mental preoccupation is not a matter of to-do lists, though they are included. Sevens' attention is on how they will experience everything they want. They say it is fun to plan whether or not the plans are carried out; it's often more fun planning than doing. It is a way of being open to all possibilities:

As long as I'm in my imagination, I'm sure that no practical detail will get in the way of my plans.

It's a kind of rolling plan – a bit like one of those architect's drawing boards that you can move forward or back – and it includes all the possible options, my whole life. Whenever something changes, I just update the plan. It does include goals, but there can be many ways of getting there...

Planning is a way of avoiding pain, and is intensified as soon as anything threatening happens: Any projected anxiety about the future and the mind starts racing. Although they seem spontaneous, they can unexpectedly baulk if a new idea or unexpected threat to the plan comes in:

---

[11] This section is an extract from *Thorsons Principles of the Enneagram* by Karen Webb, Thorsons, London, 1996. Reproduced with author's permission

The ABC of the Enneagram

We nearly split up when my wife kept criticising one of my business ventures. I couldn't admit that it was the plan, not me, she was attacking – and it did feel like an attack. All she was trying to do was warn me she had a gut feeling it would turn out to be a waste of time and money.

What Sevens find difficult

Suffering:
I'm always on the go in order to avoid it. When it comes, I move: I feel a moving target is harder to hit.

Commitment:
All my life, I've tried to leave as many options open as possible. For example, I chose to study in business school because that would leave me the maximum number of open doors when I got out. In sport it was the same thing, I did a lot of different sports at a high level, but I could never have forced myself to specialise in one.

Routine:
If you really restrict me to doing a routine job and I can't resign, I'll escape into my head: I'll imagine beaches, adventures…that's what I did in class when I was at school!

Questioning their own way of doing things:
Since in general people like me, it took some courage for me to recognise that something wasn't right inside me.

Difficulties for others

Lack of attention:
He's a real whirling dervish. You have trouble following him in his incessant frenetic dance, in his ideas. He jumps so fast from one subject to another that eventually it gets tiring.

Reliability:
He promises you the moon, so you make plans. You get organised, but he tends not to feel tied to commitments that were imposed on him. Changes of plan are the way he does business.

Focus:
Often, I wish we could just sit still and do nothing, rather than wanting to do something different every day, but my husband would rather try out his latest plan, and since he has a lot of them at once…

How you can encourage them

● Help them see that committing yourself does not have to be such a big problem.
● Be at their side when they are tempted to give up.
● Help them discover that the year has several seasons, and not just springtime.
● Help them appreciate values which are different from their own, such as rigour, focus, and perseverance.

Advantages of being a Seven

Association of ideas:
Because I have a mind that jumps about all over the place, I can quickly make interesting connections.

Cheerfulness:
People see me as a big kid, and it's the best gift anyone can give me. Knowing how to have fun all the time and everywhere is a genuine gift from God.

The ability to bounce back:
I've experienced many tricky situations, but I've always been able to find the bright side of the situation. Even after an accident or a funeral, I can find a reason to be positive.

Essential qualities

● Their light, smiling, sunny, optimistic, spontaneous and inventive personality, their contagious spark of exuberance.
● When nothing is going right, they will still find a way to raise your spirits.

Famous personalities who show us Point Seven behaviour

The character of Peter Pan. Wolfgang Amadeus Mozart, Walt Whitman, Victoria Abril, Robin Williams, Groucho Marx, Yannick Noah

How Sevens can develop

Sevens can blossom by accepting that, just as the moon has two faces, life can also have a dark side, and more precisely by:

Using the perfectionist energy of point One:
● Sevens have great ingenuity; by developing their objectivity and rigour, Sevens will add depth and the pleasure of work well done, to balance their unfocused side. This will enable them to want to get better at a particular skill, rather than continuing to flit from one thing to another.
● Self-discipline, perseverance, and self-evaluation will balance them. They will find the strength to finish what they have started.

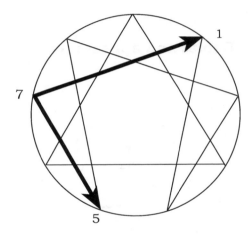

Using the observer energy of point Five:
● Taking the time to gather their sensations, to internalise their experience.
● Taking a step back, in order to digest their many experiences and to see where they are.
● Slowing down, taking stock of the situation. They will gain in depth, and take pleasure in spending time alone.

POINT EIGHT

Predominantly a Boss

You don't beg for your rights, you fight for them.
Anonymous

Habits and appearance

Eights are strong and confident in their abilities.

The ABC of the Enneagram

They know what they want and
are direct in their comments.

They like to control situations...

The ABC of the Enneagram

...and make quick decisions.

Often competitive, they like a tough opponent.

The ABC of the Enneagram

They respect strength and power...

... they impose their own rules...

They are sometimes excessive...

...and see themselves as righters
of wrong and protectors of the weak.

Understanding Eights

Eights give out a powerful energy. They make their own way in life, through their strength. They like controlling and being in charge. They often seek out confrontation, as a way of finding out others' motivations. They would rather have you against them than not know where you stand. They approach situations in an all or nothing way. When you meet them there is no confusion; what you see is what you get. They are quick to anger, and are sometimes very forceful, but it doesn't last, and once it is over, the dispute is quickly forgotten. Anger and action enable them to feel strong. They are tough and tend to be excessive.

Eights live by their instincts; the gap between impulse and action is brief.

They consider themselves to be righters of wrongs; they are always ready to defend their friends and close family, especially when they think they have been treated unfairly. They have relatively little interest in existing rules, preferring to impose their own.

They like
- Righting injustice and protecting the weak.
- Charging straight ahead.
- Fighting, winning a test of strength.

They dislike
- Lack of character.
- Softness.
- People who beat about the bush.

The Eight personality

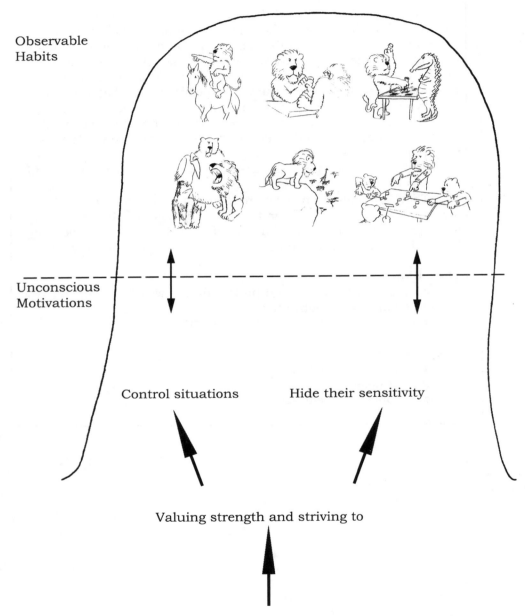

Observable
Habits

Unconscious
Motivations

Control situations   Hide their sensitivity

Valuing strength and striving to

As a child, they believed: *The world is hard and unfair; I was taken advantage of in a moment of weakness.*

The ABC of the Enneagram

Perception of the world:

As children, Eights unconsciously perceived the world as hard and unfair. Appearing weak is dangerous.

In order to compensate:

Eights chose to win respect and ensure their protection by becoming strong and by hiding their vulnerabilities.

Their system of values therefore developed around:

Strength, determination, courage, and justice.

Filters of perception were put in place:

Their attention is naturally focused on:
● Evaluating the forces involved and determining the balance of power.
● Concentrating their energy in one direction: an all or nothing style.

Their preoccupation is:
● Dominating, controlling the situation
● Initiating action, getting involved.
● Righting wrongs and protecting the weak.
● Showing their power.
● Seeking (often provocatively) the intensity of life.
● Using anger as a defence mechanism, to demand respect from others.

Their habitual defence mechanism:

Denying weakness:
I won't admit that it's possible not to achieve a result, and in order to prove it, I will force it to happen.

Under the influence of their passion

When they are afraid of appearing weak, Eights ruin their lives
with too much

Lust

They become excessive in everything, as if they have to prove they
exist: eating too much, drinking, being arrogant, with the music turned
all the way up. They get into rages that make the walls shake, and may
abuse their power.

When they control their passion

Eights can use their strength in ways other than at full volume.
They discover

Innocence

Innocence is a state of being where the world is considered safe and where it is possible to let go of your defence mechanisms. In a state of innocence, you can live without having to constantly decide what's fair and what isn't.

In this state, Eights can accept values other than brute force; they can let themselves be touched by tenderness and become capable of moderation.

Lust[12]

The Eights' emotional focus of **Lust** is not sexual, but an urgent impulsive reaching to grasp life fully: lust for life. Focusing on whatever makes them feel fully alive, they may bring as much gusto to intellectual pursuits as to 'bed, booze and board.'

> *I want a lot, and I don't understand people who are frightened – come on, it's good. I do overdo it – once you start it's hard to stop. Zero-100 is easy, but cruising at 55 is hard. I can get excessive about diets too – it's good for me and I just go for it – while I do!*

Their great capacity for sensate experience also defuses their energy:

> *I've a great capacity for not getting the essential things done, or even little things like putting up a shelf – I'd much rather do some gardening or whatever.*

Vengeance focuses on injustice and redressing the balance. Seeing the world in black and white, believing themselves to be right, Eights assign blame and direct the force of their anger towards righting the wrong. They will ensure the punishment fits the crime, and can go to great lengths to do so.

What Eights find difficult

__I have trouble taking orders__, especially when I don't respect the authority figure who gives them. I prefer taking things into my own hands.

Some days, I want to show tenderness, but it's like I've forgotten how to do it.

__When I explode, I don't realise how disturbing it can be for others__. I like others to express themselves, to say what's on their mind. But, if they know that I might explode, they hesitate to say what they really think. It took me years to understand the need to be tactful, even to treat people with kid gloves.

---

[12] This section is an extract from *Thorsons Principles of the Enneagram* by Karen Webb, Thorsons, London, 1996. Reproduced with author's permission.

The ABC of the Enneagram

Difficulties for others

He always needs to oppose, to be against what you say. Most of the time, it's a sort of game. He's just testing your motivation. All he's interested in is testing your mettle, your commitment to what you're saying. In this mood, he can be verbally aggressive; it's a sort of provocation that enables him to know where you stand. Like the rest of his behaviour, it can be excessive, and some days, it gets exhausting.

How you can encourage them

- Appreciate them in the moments when they are themselves, when they open themselves up to their sensitivity.
- Help them notice some of their excesses and the intensity of their impulses.
- Show them that there are other options besides force.
- Help them realise their effect on others can be intimidating.
- Say what you think, don't hide anything; it's important that everything that has to be said is said.
- Help them understand that virtues other than strength are important to you.

Advantages of being an Eight

I can get everything I want. I never give up. Even if they tell me no, it doesn't matter, I'll do it my way, with no concession to others.

Essential Qualities

- Eights show us the ability to decide, to resolve things. They also have a formidable sense of what's the right decision to take.
- They know what they think and are ready to fight to defend it.
- They are a blessing for their friends, who are like members of their tribe. They are ready to defend and protect them.
- They will do everything to right injustice, whatever law is in force.

Famous personalities who show us Point Eight behaviour

Golda Meir, Louis XIV of France, Ludwig van Beethoven, G.I. Gurdjieff, Charles de Gaulle, John Wayne, Helmut Kohl, Sarah Ferguson, Bette Midler

How Eights can develop

Eights can blossom by finding their inner child, and more precisely by:

Using the altruist energy of point Two:
● By developing their ability to put themselves in others' shoes, they will discover the idea of empathy, instead of continuing to want to dominate.
● They will improve their communication, opening themselves up to others and letting them see their vulnerability. They will become more engaging when they get back in touch with the compassion that is inside them.

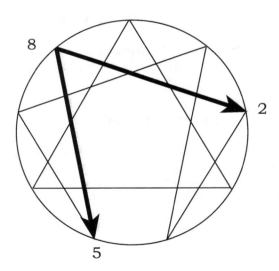

The ABC of the Enneagram

Using the observer energy of point Five:

● The Five energy will give them a transfusion of coolness into their hot blood.

● The ability to think objectively, even in situations when their anger rises, will give them a clear coherent overview of situations.

● Developing their inner life will enable them to observe themselves and reflect before they come to a conclusion, instead of always reacting in the heat of the moment.

POINT NINE

Predominantly a Mediator

Haste makes waste
Anonymous

Habits and appearance

Nines have a soothing presence.

The ABC of the Enneagram

...they have a routine...

...and they are good listeners.

The ABC of the Enneagram

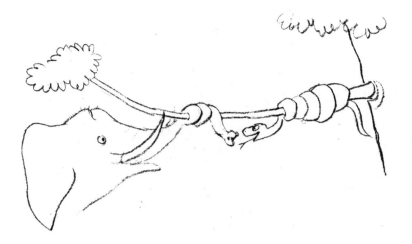

They seek harmony.

As mediators, they try to avoid conflict and confrontation.

The ABC of the Enneagram

Indecisive, they have trouble making choices...

...and they find it hard to form an opinion.

The ABC of the Enneagram

They hate being under pressure...

...and they prefer living at their own pace.

The ABC of the Enneagram

Understanding Nines

Nines seek harmony and avoid conflicts. They create a calm and tranquil atmosphere around themselves. They have a special relationship with nature. They have a routine and believe that you have to give things time.

They are conciliatory and instinctively know how to put themselves in others' shoes, to the point of sometimes forgetting what they want themselves. When they study the Enneagram, Nines often identify with each of the types. They recognise that all points of view are valid. They are absent-minded, and often have trouble differentiating between what is important and what isn't.

They need time to make a decision. Making a choice is always difficult and is sometimes experienced as giving up a part of themselves. In order to avoid difficult choices, they lock themselves into a routine. Conflict terrifies them because it can lead to separation, which is painful. They tend to let the situation get worse rather than face a potential explosion.

They like:
- Tranquillity, harmony, and comfort.
- Nature.
- A certain routine, stable schedules.
- Compromise.
- Listening to you.
- Taking the time to experience life.

They dislike:
- Having to take a stand.
- Having to fight.
- Saying no.
- Feeling your impatience.

The Nine personality

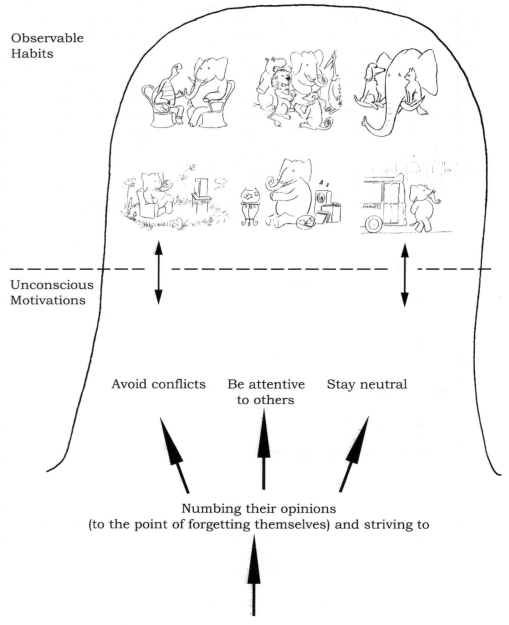

Observable
Habits

Unconscious
Motivations

Avoid conflicts   Be attentive   Stay neutral
to others

Numbing their opinions
(to the point of forgetting themselves) and striving to

As a child, they believed:
The world rejects me when I express my opinion.

The ABC of the Enneagram

Perception of the world:

As children, Nines unconsciously perceived that they were not listened to. Expressing their opinion can be a source of conflict and separation.

In order to compensate:

Nines chose to let things run their course, letting people forget about them, and merging with their surroundings, to the point of forgetting themselves. With time, things will sort themselves out without friction.

Their system of values therefore developed around:

Peace, patience, restraint, and paying attention to others.

Filters of perception were put in place:

They focused on:
- Maintaining harmony.
- Being attentive and agreeable to others.
- Dissipating their energy in attending to secondary tasks.

Their preoccupation is:

- Avoiding conflicts, staying neutral.
- Not saying no or taking a position that is too definite.
- Understanding others (to the point of merging with them).
- Maintaining a peaceful life: habits are reassuring.
- Letting things pass, containing anger when it arises: it could lead to separation.

Their habitual defence mechanism:

Stubbornness, inertia, and non-action.

Under the influence of their passion

When they are afraid of conflict, Nines ruin their lives with too much

Sloth

In this state, Nines become indifferent. They busy themselves with everything and nothing in order to forget that they actually fundamentally disagree with whatever is at stake, but they prefer to keep quiet. They are unable to act because of their fear of conflict:

When I go into my spiral of not wanting to express myself, I find a way to justify my non-action and I stubbornly take refuge in it.

For a long time, I thought that merging with someone was achieving supreme unity. Therefore, I expressed my opinion less and less, in order to achieve this union.

The ABC of the Enneagram

When they control their passion

Nines continue to prefer listening to others, but they manage to express their opinion. They are in a state of

Right action

Instead of looking for the spur to action in the outside world, I started to understand that I have to find it in myself. Instead of focusing on trivial things in order to distract myself from my fear of separation, I now understand that, at any moment, I have the ability within me to do the right thing; I exist as an individual.

With this discovery, comes the awareness of love. Love is a state in which Nines realise that they don't need to deny their existence or forget themselves. They exist as individuals, and so they are loveable, just as they are.

Sloth [13]

The energy capacity of Nines is dissolved by their sloth, which prevents them from existing for their own sake and committing themselves.

Sloth and indolence are inwardly focused, not outwardly, and support self-forgetting. The emotional focus of sloth keeps Nines disconnected from their own emotions, particularly the physical impulse of anger. They replace them with a gut-level awareness of others' moods and feelings which is so immediate it is as though they 'become' the other person whilst in their presence.

Nines can break through sloth by discovering their anger, but usually they feel:

It's not worth it, who am I to be angry at this, I'm not sure I even am angry.

If acknowledged, it will probably be volcanic, and displaced:

I'm not sure what I'm angry about, but I am angry and you may have something to do with it.

If they feel pushed to make a firm statement about their own wishes or boundaries – that is, to remember themselves – anger rises which they can disown by blaming someone else for forcing them to be angry:

It feels like driving with both feet down – one on the accelerator and on the brake – it's very frustrating. And there's an internal rage which I can't express and often don't feel, but other people do, and ask me if I'm angry, and it's: No, but I will be if you keep asking.

Activity may stop when Nines start to question their self-forgetting and search for who they are apart from 'an echo and reflection of other people.'

Inertia is also part of the mental preoccupation of indolence. It is a form of self-neglect in which, caught between things that have to be done or unable to decide which of their many personal priorities to pursue, they cannot motivate themselves to choose and act on their choice. Nines are indolent towards their essential priorities to the extent that they often say they have not planned to be where they are in life, it just 'sort of happened.'

I need a structure to keep me on track, and usually that's provided by another person because I find it difficult to do that for myself. The temptation is to find an interesting structure and just go with that.

---

[13] This section is an extract from *Thorsons Principles of the Enneagram* by Karen Webb, Thorsons, London, 1996. Reproduced with author's permission

The ABC of the Enneagram

They also 'space out,' burdened not only by the many things they could do, but by their very way of paying attention. Wishing to include everything, they can think about many different things at once. What someone looks like, their feelings, their ideas, and what they are saying are all overlaid on Nines' existing thoughts, and rather than focus on one they distance themselves mentally.

Nines avoid acknowledging indolence, and cut off the enormous physical energy which threatens to overwhelm them, by 'narcotising' – numbing themselves with repetitive and compulsive inessential activities. This can be as simple as reading or computer games, but may be anything that helps them to forget the pain of forgetting.

What Nines find difficult

Setting priorities:

I often have trouble distinguishing between what's important and what isn't: I find myself watering the plants and washing the floor when what I intended to do was move the armchair in the living room.

Making choices:

When I studied the Enneagram, I identified with each of the types. There, as elsewhere in my life, I understand all points of view, but I don't want to have to choose.

Believe it or not, but I have never started a relationship. What I mean is, I never chose to start a relationship. I let people and things come to me, rather than going towards them. In all the emotional relationships I've had, it was always the other person who made the first move.

Taking action in emergencies:

I'm incapable of hurrying. That's why I have so many routines. My entire day is organised so I can take my time. The more I'm told: Hurry up, the less I'm able to act quickly.

Difficulties for others

One of my daughters is like this. She lives at her own pace. She starts out by merging with a place before being interested what people say. First of all she has to feel physically in harmony with a place, before she can start to think logically. On first impression, she seems to be a bit slow. But it's like the force of inertia, once she gets going, she's reliable and steadfast.

He has his own pace. If we need to go faster because we'll be late, he gets stubborn. In everyday life, he has his routines. They enable him to ensure that he can do everything at his own pace. When something unexpected happens, the pressure makes him slow down rather than speed up.

How you can encourage them

- Help them to pay attention to themselves, to define their desires, to know what they want.
- Help them notice their own point of view.
- Help them take risks.
- Make them establish an order of priorities and help them follow it.
- Value their form of quiet intelligence.

Advantages of being a Nine

I'm a university professor and my students never give me any trouble because I have about me a quiet strength that they respect. The same thing happens at home; people tell me I give out a soothing energy.
I think I'm much less sensitive to stress than others.

Essential Qualities

This combination of peace and stubbornness makes Nines easygoing. Their listening skills and restraint are unsurpassed. They teach us to put things and time in perspective, to live in harmony with ourselves, with our environment, and with nature.

- Patience: They know how to take the time they need, in all areas.
- The notion of unselfish love: They take genuine pleasure in putting themselves in your shoes, accepting you the way you are.
- Peace: Their pace of life, which is relatively slow, often helps others to feel calm.

The ABC of the Enneagram

Famous personalities who show us Point Nine behaviour

The Dalai Lama, Carl Jung, Grace Kelly, Juliette Binoche, Pete Sampras, Alfred Hitchcock, Luciano Pavarotti.

The role of Peter Falk in Columbo.

How Nines can develop

The fighting spirit of point Three can give them:
● Clarification in their position: knowing where they stand.
● Better management of priorities: making choices, deciding on an option, defending themselves and putting themselves centre stage when necessary.

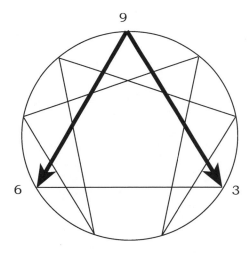

The loyalist energy of Point Six will give them:
● The courage to take risks. They can find the strength to question the way they do things, and to be themselves.
● The courage to claim their place, instead of continuing to be self-effacing.
● The ability to see beyond appearances, to show more realism.

The ABC of the Enneagram

The ABC of the Enneagram

PART THREE

Practical Applications

I heard the common call of all spiritual quests: Awake sleeper, awake. For you must die to yourself in order to be reborn at a higher level of Being.

Louis Pauwels

The challenge in recognising your type

Having the honesty to recognise yourself in a type is really means accepting yourself the way you are. This step is the first level of all development: Krishnamurti said, 'Virtue begins with self-knowledge'. But it's a difficult step, one that demands a certain amount of humility, as this old Hindi tale illustrates.

The Blind Men and the Elephant

Once there were six blind men from Hindustan
Educated and curious,
They wanted to meet an elephant for the first time,
In order to advance their knowledge.

The first approached the elephant,
And when he slid up against his huge solid flank
He exclaimed: God bless me,
An elephant is like a wall!

The second, feeling a tusk,
Cried, Oh, Oh!
Round, smooth, and pointed?
In my opinion, this elephant
Is just like a spear!

The Third headed towards the elephant,
Took his undulating trunk
In his hands and said:
For me, the elephant is like a snake!

The Fourth stretched out his impatient hand,
And feeling its knee
Was convinced that an elephant
Resembled a tree!

The ABC of the Enneagram

The Fifth grabbed its ear by chance and said:
Even for the blindest of the blind
This wonderful elephant
Is just like a fan!

The Sixth felt his way along the elephant,
And grabbing its tail which was sweeping the air,
Recognised something familiar,
I see, he said, the elephant
is like a rope!

Then the six blind men,
Talked passionately for a long time,
Each falling into one exaggeration or another,
For, although each held a part of the truth,
They were all mistaken!

Here is another example, from an American novel written at the turn of the 20th century:

Until that moment, I lived in my childhood universe like a fish in the ocean. I thought it was the only world that existed, the only possible world. Now, for the first time, I've grasped the existence of a world outside myself.

As we mentioned earlier, it is not easy to identify our different facets, especially when there is some interference from other areas of our consciousness, such as:

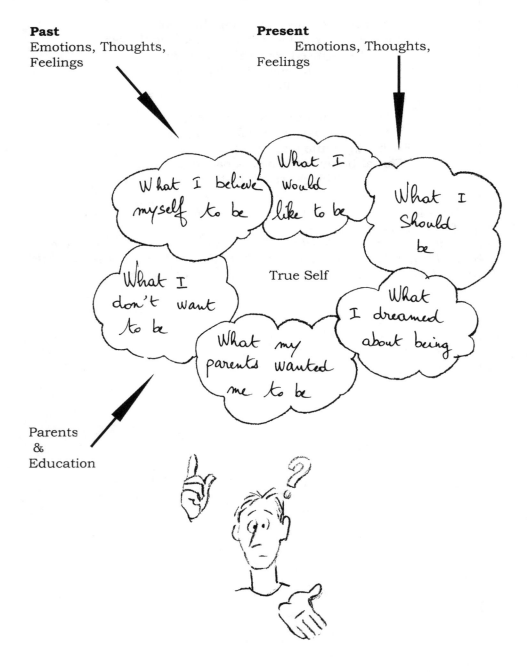

Past
Emotions, Thoughts, Feelings

Present
Emotions, Thoughts, Feelings

What I believe myself to be

What I would like to be

What I should be

True Self

What I don't want to be

What my parents wanted me to be

What I dreamed about being

Parents & Education

The ABC of the Enneagram

The necessary steps in the search for the 'true self', are well described in this extract from the *Pierre des Sages*[14]:

> We have to learn how to lower ourselves, to bend down, to make ourselves small in order to enter the chamber of the soul. Seeing ourselves as we truly are demands a certain humility; it involves passing through a narrow door, leaving behind on the doorstep our sense of our own importance, tearing ourselves away from this image of ourselves which is so pleasant to us, and which we try to maintain at all costs... The spiritual journey is not about wrapping life up in disguises, in deceptive costumes, in colourful or pleasant garments. It demands first of all that we should be honest with ourselves, noticing our thoughts, emotions, and passions without judging them, recognising honestly, for example, how a criticism leads to an irritated reaction, and why. Only in this way can we learn to decode this automatic mechanism which enslaves us.

Exploring Type with other people

This book offers a first approach to understanding personality types. Workshops enable us to draw more subtle distinctions; we can talk about similarities between people without lapsing into caricature and saying: this type always reacts like this, that one, like that. Workshops enable us to have a living and personalised approach. We can take the time to let each person discover their dominant type at their own pace.

Workshops also enable us to help people distinguish between certain types that look alike superficially. The most common confusions are between points One and Six, Two and Nine, Three and Seven, Five and Nine. Some people also hesitate between two neighbouring types, for example, between points Five and Six.

To summarise, when people first encounter the Enneagram, they tend to fall into one of three groups:

● Those who recognise themselves in one type to such an extent that they find it unsettling to notice how much the description is like them.

● Those who can see themselves in two or three types and what to know more.

● Those that recognise themselves in all types, and don't identify with any particular type.

---

[14] Antoine Kerlys, Éditions Terre Blanche, 7, rue Émile-Barry, Toulouse, p. 22.

In almost all cases, people recognise themselves in one type by the end of the third day of a workshop, especially with the help of other participants. Although the group leader may feel they recognise a person's type very quickly, they won't say anything, because it is important to allow everyone the time to discover themselves for themselves. However, the leader may guide people in their search.

Conducting the search for your type within a group is all the more interesting because you can ask questions of people who have already identified their type, and this enables you to ask yourself whether or not you behave like them.

Limitations Of The System

Those who have worked with the Enneagram for a long time are unanimous in saying that its biggest danger is that it works too well. Often, people who have had a quick introduction to the system think they know it, and confidently make judgements about others. There are several pitfalls that it is important to avoid:

Forgetting that there isn't a good or bad type

Although our society values the image of some types more than others, we must not fall into the trap of valuing some individuals more than others.

Wanting to identify levels of 'development' within a type

'I know a Three who isn't very aware, he's still in a state of vanity!'

As we've just said, we must remember that each human being has their own inner beauty, their own difficulties, and who am I to dare judge who is an aware Three and who is less aware?

Identifying someone's type but forgetting that each person is unique

When we start to talk about Ones and Twos it's important to remember that actually, we're talking about a unique individual, whose dominant personality characteristic is in type X.

Forgetting that it's not as simple as that

Even if knowing about personality types greatly facilitates understanding others, human beings remain infinitely rich and variable. It's good to remember that millions of people have the same type (about 600 million) but that within those millions, the variations are infinite.

The ABC of the Enneagram

Forgetting that the Enneagram is only a means to an end

Systems like the Enneagram are only a means of connecting more deeply with yourself and with others. In the end, type isn't as important as the help it gives us to deepen our understanding of ourselves and of close friends and family. Observable habits are only appearance. Even though behaviour may enable us to discover the dominant type of a person, what really matters is the heart, the soul of each person, and what we really are, deep inside.

Intellectualising the system

A system is only a system. People are dynamic and infinitely variable. In a book, there is no way that we can truly capture the energies and emotions of every individual. This energy, this living quality of each individual, tells us just as much about their inner beauty as any intellectual study we may undertake. The energy of each type has something special, a specific flavour, but we need to learn to listen to it with our heart as well as our head.

Only with a living teaching method, which takes into account the different dimensions of the human being and conveys it in an atmosphere of immense respect for human nature, can we avoid these pitfalls. This form of teaching exists. It is called the oral tradition. We've dedicated a chapter to it later in this book.

Potential Applications of the Enneagram

They are infinite. Our students have found the Enneagram helpful in couple relationships, children's education, and professional life in all its forms. Teachers, speech therapists, lawyers, shopkeepers, sports coaches, nurses, nursery nurses, choreographers, writers, craftspeople, salespeople, and of course, psychologists and team leaders all find the Enneagram useful. We also work with heads of companies and religious leaders.

In this book, we have chosen to concentrate on personal development rather than work-based applications, because personal development was the original application of the Enneagram. We now move on to explore some aspects of personal development in more detail, namely:
- The work of transformation
- Teaching according to the oral tradition
- The historical development of the Enneagram.

The Work of Transformation

Once the passion is named, the work of transformation begins: converting passion into virtue. This involves constant self-observation: 'Am I in automatic mode, under the influence of my personality, or am I connecting with my true Self, aware of the present moment?'

Self-observation consists of stopping from time to time during the day in order to watch our minds function and to take notice of our repeating patterns, noticing the tenacity with which certain preoccupations impose themselves on our mind. Only self-observation can teach us our dominant passion. If we don't do this, more often than not we will confuse our type with what we'd like it to be.

The mere fact of observing our habits of thought with detachment, makes these habits less automatic. The benefits of this transformation vary between individuals, but current research on the Enneagram leads us to think that our patterns of thought consume a good part of our daily energy. If we can observe these habits from a neutral space – as a conscious observer – we will find strategies to intervene, ways of modifying these repeating patterns. Thus we will free up the energy that was previously used up in automatic responses.

This work of transformation or alchemy, that lasts a lifetime on different levels, is called Holy war in many cultures. The archetypal images of knights fighting a dragon (Saint George, Saint Michael,...) are actually representations of Man liberating himself from his ego.

Helen Palmer has this to say on the subject:[15]

> The Enneagram is part of a teaching tradition that views personality preoccupations as teachers, or indicators of latent abilities that unfold during the development of higher consciousness. The diagrams that appear in this book are a partial view of a more complete model that descries the levels of humanity's possible evolution from personality through a range of unusual human potentials, such as empathy, omniscience, and love. It is vital that this larger context not be overlooked by focusing attention on the nine character traits, because the complete Enneagram is one of the very few models of consciousness that addresses the relationship between personality and other levels of human capability. The power of the system lies in the fact that ordinary patterns of personality, those very habits of heart and mind that we tend to dismiss as merely neurotic, are seen as potential access points into higher states of awareness.

---

[15] Helen Palmer, *The Enneagram*, Ed. Harper Collins, p. 3-4

We can easily recognise the value of the Enneagram that describes personality because a great deal of our attention is focused on the thoughts and feelings that we identify as our self. If, however, our own unique personality, or what each of us thinks or as myself, is in fact only one aspect in a continuum of human development, then our own thoughts and feelings must in some way constitute a staging ground for understanding the next phase of our own unfolding.

We intend to explore this theme in a future work.

The Oral Tradition[16]

Seeing and hearing representatives of the same type talking about what they are is probably the best way of conveying the power of this tool and of protecting yourself against some of the dangers mentioned above.

David Daniels, professor of Psychology at Stanford University, has this to say about the oral tradition approach:

> Founded by Claudio Naranjo in 1970, the oral tradition is based on living accounts of representatives of each type. It's not about passing knowledge on from generation to generation, even though this is the original meaning of the expression. In fact, it's the representatives of the same type who reveal their own story, in the context of a panel. (small group of people of the same type agreeing to testify together)
>
> This enables you to hear personal observations and everyday preoccupations directly, and to see the characteristics of each type. The oral tradition is probably the best way to teach the Enneagram. It offers all the advantages: it brings the system to life, it allows listeners to more easily identify the type to which they belong and to better appreciate the differences.

Helen Palmer makes the following points about the value of panels[17]:

> Seeing and hearing a group of articulate and willing people express a similar point of view transmits far more of the power of the system than can possibly be transmitted by mere written record of their words. After about an hour, a group of people who start out looking physically very different begin to seem the same. The viewer can sense the similarities in physical holding patterns, emotion tone, the tension points in the face, and the quality of personal emanation that are the more subtle signs of type. The auditorium fills with a definite presence ad the character unfolds. There is a unique feel to each of the types, a distinguishing quality, a presence in the hall.

---

[16] Throughout the world: fax (1) 510 540 7626
[17] Helen Palmer, *The Enneagram*, Ed. Harper Collins, p 4-5

A group of the same type can initially appear to have nothing in common, because the viewer is paying attention to their differences in sex, age, race, profession, and personal style. Within an hour, however, they begin to look the same: their histories, their choices, their preferences, their goals. What they avoid and what they dream begin to seem the same. They even start to look alike, once your attention shifts from the surface feature of apparel and a personable smile.

The world looks very different to each of the nine, and by lending yourself to the way that others feel within themselves, you can shift out of your own point of view into a true understanding of who the people in your life really are, rather than what your ideas about them might lead you to believe.

In practice, a workshop is about creating an open atmosphere and a non-judgmental stance, and then allowing participants to take the floor. Regular periods of reflection enable us to create a true atmosphere of respect for the human quality of people's testimony, which is absolutely essential if you want to enable the true physical expression, turns of phrase, and fundamental qualities of each type to be expressed.

The ABC of the Enneagram

PART FOUR

The History of the Enneagram

On the road of people who desire to be wise, there are nine secret doors.

Giordano Bruno, Venice, 1580

A Note on this Chapter

This chapter leads us to the heart of the Enneagram, to learning about its original purpose. Its interest is thus twofold: to discover its origins and at the same time to understand its connection with higher levels of consciousness, which were discussed earlier. It's impossible to encompass the complete history of the Enneagram in a few pages. We can offer you sketches of the most important figures, but there are many more. We've chosen to concentrate on the most ancient two: Pythagoras and Evagrius Ponticus.

Pythagoras

Drawing based on the sculpture 'Greek man' by Auguste Rodin.

The life of Pythagoras

When it comes to transpersonal or psychospiritual psychology, Pythagoras is the father figure.

At a time when science, spirituality, and psychology were still connected, Pythagoras was able to study with priests who held this knowledge. Fascinated by the human soul and its evolution, he spent thirty years of his life learning about techniques of spiritual development in Thebes and Babylon.

Believing that all religions were only a fragment of the same Truth, he created a school of psychological and spiritual development which strove for enlightenment, and where paying attention to your inner life was emphasised.

In the school of Pythagoras, the students' first task was to conquer their passions. This step is the thread that connects all the great figures in the history of the Enneagram.

At a time when all teaching was communicated orally, geometric figures were commonly used, if only as a teaching aid. Pythagoras developed ten geometric figures symbolising the first ten numbers. Later, they were called the ten seals of Pythagoras.

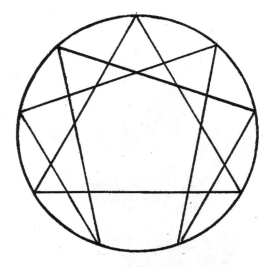

The Enneagram is the ninth of the ten seals of Pythagoras

The Pythagorean school

First of all, the Pythagorean approach involved developing the inner life through silence, asceticism, and discipline. The method consisted of mastering the body, emotions, and mind. The ultimate goal was to become free, meaning being able to live each moment fully, in harmony with the universe.

In this school, the teaching of mathematics went hand in hand with music, astronomy, philosophy and wisdom. Much emphasis was placed on the importance of listening: listening to silence, listening to your inner cacophony, listening to others. Pythagoras considered that his era put too much stress on the mind and that:

dialectic and reasoning without awareness only lead to empty heads[18].

---

[18] *Les Grands Initiés*, by E. Schuré, Perrin, 1960.

The importance of Nine: the nine muses

The symbolism of the number nine is especially important, because nine is the highest stage of development that Man can reach, ten being the number of God. (This idea is also found in the Hebrew Kabbalah, where the highest sephiroth of the Tree of Life, Kether, is inaccessible to human understanding).

Pythagoras only passed on this knowledge about numbers, letters, or geometric figures to those who were successfully admitted to the novitiate. According to Edward Schuré:[19]

> Pythagoras used to teach in the temple of the Muses. Inside this circular temple, you could see the nine Muses in marble. Standing in the centre was Hestia watching, wrapped in a veil, solemn and mysterious. For the Greeks, as for the Romans, Hestia or Vesta was the guardian of the divine principle present in all things.

In fact, these muses were the symbols of nine universal energies, which also represent nine facets of ourselves, and these nine base energies were also symbolically present in the nine numbers.

In many fields, Pythagoras' thinking remained a point of reference for centuries; his theory of harmonics would guide Kepler in his work to describe the structure of the solar system in the 17th century and would lead to the discoveries of Newton.

This sacred mathematics therefore had a logic to it, even if today the idea of giving a symbolic value to numbers seems strange to our Cartesian minds.

The origins of the diagram

According to Fernand Schwartz[21] :

> We are familiar with mysterious and initiatory experiences through art, philosophy, and the Mysteries. Thus, poets like Homer, or tragedians and philosophers, like Pythagoras, Heraclitus and Plato, hid the principles of things; they conveyed the truth in the form of enigmas, symbols, allegories, and figures. The oracles of Delphi also expressed themselves in an indirect and mysterious way. That is why the founders of the Mysteries, who were also philosophers, initiated in the highest levels of Truth, expressed their doctrines through a symbolic and mythical language. In this way, initiated people veiled the heart of the Truth from the eyes of the rest of the world. They protected the sacred.

---

[19] *Les Grands Initiés,* p.18
[20] *La Tradition et les Voies de la Connaissance,* éditions NADP, 1987, p. 15.
[21] *Der Himmerl beginnt in Dir,* Herderbücherei, 1994, p.10.

The seals of Pythagoras were probably an example of this symbolic language.

It appears therefore that the Enneagram originally had several objectives:

- To symbolise in a simple teaching tool, powerful truths about human nature.
- To pass on a tool for personal development, based on the number nine, which is synonymous with ultimate enlightenment and bliss.
- Using the same model, to communicate facts; about physics, mathematices or even energy.
- To show that the great laws of the universe are always valid, both at the human level (microcosm) and at the level of the universe (macrocosm).
- To keep certain information secret.

After Pythagoras' death, some of his close friends and family continued his teaching. The philosophy of these Pythagoreans influenced many religious tradition, as well as the first Christian monks, who were known as the Desert Fathers, one of whom was **Evagrius Ponticus.**

The Desert Fathers

In 350 AD, Anthony, an Egyptian of wealthy origins, decided to renounce everything and live apart from people, in the desert, not only to search for the God inside him, but above all to find himself. He would confront his shadows. It was to be a struggle against his demon, against the forces of the unconscious, and was as hard as a struggle against wild beasts.

He was a Christian, and came from a tradition stretching back to Egypt and Alexandria, at the beginning of the 2nd century AD. He used withdrawal, silence, and meditation as means of dissolving personality. As well as renouncing social life and nature, and enduring inhuman living conditions, his school also involved breaking with all the habits and systems making up secular social life.

The example of St. Anthony led to a school, and soon hundreds of seekers came to share this ascetic way of life. The first generations lived completely alone. Later, those who arrived were taken in charge by the older ones and, little by little, congregations formed around an abba or spiritual father. (Abba has several meanings: Father, priest, and more generally 'abbot')

Anselm Grün, a contemporary Benedictine monk specialising in this period of Christian history, writes[22]:

> Most of the thought and practices of the Desert Fathers resembled those of the Pythagoreans: their organisation, the connection between asceticism and mysticism... In addition, much of their vocabulary is of Greek origin: anachorèse, monachos[23]...

They focused on the same values: inner life, asceticism, silence, analysis of thought and feelings, the fight against the passions and above all, the certainty that a direct connection with God is attainable.

If you take a psychological view of their discoveries, they can be summarised thus:

- I am responsible for my suffering, because I created the patterns of beliefs that make me suffer.
- Happiness comes from becoming aware of what I am (self-knowledge), the acceptance of what I am, and initiating change.

---

[22] *Der Himmel beginnt in Dir*, Herderucherei, 1944, p10
[23] For 'monk', originally, a man who lives alone

Who were the Desert Fathers?

The majority were Egyptians of peasant origins; the only thing they had in common was this search for the truth deep inside themselves. They believed that without superior self-knowledge, believers ran the risk that their concept of God was no more than pure projection.

Among them, one figure is particularly interesting, because he structured this psycho-spiritual search and formed the idea of the seven deadly sins, from which come the passions of the Enneagram.

Evagrius Ponticus (345-399)

He was born Greek (in what is present-day Georgia, on the Black Sea). He was a theologian, and was therefore particularly well educated. For personal reasons he left Constantinople and civilisation for the Egyptian desert. After being initiated into solitary life in the desert under the wing of an elder, he quickly became a central figure. Many brothers came to him for advice for their inner fight. Palladios, one of his students, said of him:

> The brothers used to gather around him on Saturday and Sunday. All night they would share their troubles with him, respecting the power of his words, and they came back full of joy and thanking God, because, truly, his words were just (Book 48).

Evagrius has a special place in the history of the Desert Fathers; he was the first of the Desert Fathers to write his ideas down. Some of his writings still exist, two of which concern us especially: *Praktikos* and *Chapters on Prayer*. We find there, in fact, an important element of the origins of the Enneagram, that is to say:
- A symbol which is very like the Enneagram
- The eight evil thoughts which would later become the Christian seven deadly sins.

Two contemporary authors are especially interested in Evagrius:
- Anselm Grün, a German Benedictine monk who teaches theology and meditation techniques[24].
- John Eudes Bamberger, Abbot of a Trappist monastery in the state of New York[25].

---

[24] Author of *Geistliche Begleitung bei den Wüstenvätern*, Münsterswarzach 1992, *Der Himmel beginnt in Dir*, Herderb Bücherei 1994.]
[25] Author of the series *Cistercian Studies*, Kalamazoo, Michigan, 1978.

The ABC of the Enneagram

Evagrius, father of the seven deadly sins

Evagrius developed – among other concepts – a list of eight vices or distracting thoughts, and in one of his writings (*De vittis, quae opposita sunt virtutibus*), he actually lists nine.[26] Evagrius also gives information on the dynamics between the types:

> I first need to recognise my type in order to be able to attack my vice – all other paths are mere illusions. I have to observe where my energy flows, what blocks me, and what blinds me. The source of my greatest weakness is also the source of my most important gift. Through my passion, I can discover my main talent, and then my passion will be transformed and I will be able to enable the divine fruit that I have inside of me to flower.

Evagrius and the Enneagram

In the writings of Evagrius, one text mentions a figure combining a triangle, hexagon, and a sphere[27]. In another text, Evagrius mentions nine passions, nine paths of distraction, nine ways to losing your centre: anger, pride, the search for glory or vanity, sadness and envy, avarice, gluttony, lust, and sloth. Except for certain allusions in Dante's *Divine Comedy*, nothing comes closer to the Enneagram in all the known literature since that time. It appears therefore that the Enneagram is a connection between Antiquity, the first Christians, and the Sufi culture[28]. It gives us pause for thought to notice how different religions, which are so distant from each other today, intermixed actively at that time.

---

[26] The parallel with the passions of the Enneagram (rediscovered by Ichazo in 1970) is almost complete with one exception: fear is missing in point Six while in point Four envy and sadness are mentioned simultaneously.]

[27] This text is part of the introduction of a book by Evagrius: *Chapters on Prayer*. Evagrius interprets the triangle as a symbol of the trinity, an expression for faith, hope, and love. In recent development of the Enneagram, these three virtues are most often attributed to the three points of the triangle: faith for Six (head), hope for Three (heart), and love for the Nine (belly).

[28] Reminder: the figure of the Enneagram came to us from Sufism, see the following page.

Finally, Lynn Quirolo[29] traces a link through Pythagoras and Evagrius to Gurdjieff:

> In the 4th century writing of Evagrius Ponticus we find a highly developed contemplative psychology which has become all but extinct in the West. We also find a Pythagorean interpretation of an important Biblical symbolic number[30]. Fragments of both this psychology and its symbolism are found in the teaching of Gurdjieff and Ouspensky. As these ideas were part of the Hellenistic 'warp' of the fabric of Christian and Islamic religions, we find striking similarities between early Christian thought and the later Sufi spirituality and cosmology.

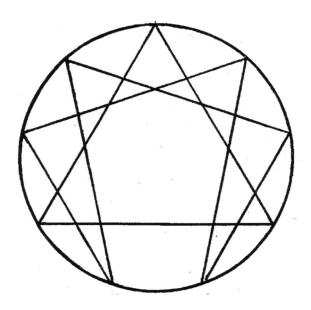

---

[29] Extract from *The Enneagram Monthly*, May 1996.
[30] The number 153, which Saint Augustine and Saint Jerome were also analysing.

Other Contributors to the System

Sufism

Sufism was born two centuries later, in the same geographical area where the Desert Fathers lived. Sufism can be thought of as the mystical tradition of Islam. Dealing with the relationship between Sufism and the Enneagram could potentially fill one or even several books. We hope to deal with this subject in a future work.

Sufism is based on several key elements, one of which is the Jihad: the Holy war...against the ego. The only aspects of Sufi culture that are common knowledge are the dance of the whirling dervishes and calligraphy. If you look a bit further, you will find in Sufism the same fundamental principles as in the Pythagorean school: self-knowledge and self-observation, experience of the present moment: the divine presence in the accomplishment of every action, the harmonious relationship with the universe, the physical and artistic aspects, the symbolism of numbers, and meditation. One thing is certain: Sufi culture used the diagram and the theory of the passions in a form which was very different from the Christian notions of sin or passion.

The Sufi figure that has come down to us is a little more complex than the Pythagoreans' diagram and is called 'wajh Allah' or 'the Sign of Divine presence'.

Dante and Chaucer

The theory of the passions is found again in the 14th century in the work of Dante (Florence, author of the *Divine Comedy*[31]) and in the 15th century in the work of Chaucer[32] (considered to be the greatest English poet and philosopher before Shakespeare, author of the *Canterbury Tales).*

---

[31] The *Divine Comedy* is considered to be a major work of humanity. The *Encyclopedia Britannica* expresses it thus: Dante's *Divine Comedy,* a great work of medieval literature, is a profound Christian vision of man's temporal and eternal destiny. On its most personal level, it draws on the poet's own experience of exile from his native city of Florence; on its most comprehensive level, it may be read as an allegory, taking the form of a journey through hell, purgatory, and paradise. The poem amazes by its array of learning, its penetrating and comprehensive analysis of contemporary problems, and its inventiveness of language and imagery. The names of the nine circles of hell are those of the nine passions of the Enneagram.

[32] For Chaucer, each sin corresponds to a remedy: virtue. Thus sobriety and moderation serve to balance gluttony, compassion serves as the antidote to avarice...

For the first time here, we find, lay authors talking about the idea that each passion relates to a fundamental quality. We find in Dante's *Divine Comedy* nine main ways in which individuals can make the choice to struggle against their passion and raise themselves toward the nine steps of heaven or take the easy way and succumb to the nine circles of hell.

Gurdjieff (1877-1949)

A philosopher and writer, Gurdjieff was born in Alexandropol, on the Black Sea. His province, which up to that time had been Ottoman, had, at the time of his birth, just been conquered by the armies of the Tsar.

George Ivanovich Gurdjieff came into contact very early on with different religions and cultures. He travelled to Asia Minor, from where he brought back the Enneagram (see *Rencontres avec des Hommes remarquables*).

His dream was to connect the wisdom of the east with that of the west. It seems that Gurdjieff was educated in and influenced by three major traditions: the Orthodox church, Sufism, and the Tibetan tradition. He was the first in Europe to teach using the diagram, the term Enneagram, and the link with behaviour. He used the Enneagram to show his students the point to which their fixation took control of their free will. He was the first to apply the diagram to self-knowledge. He helped his students to transcend their fixations and their ego, but he never specifically taught about the Enneagram as such.

His students were famous people from all over the world: doctors, literary critics… mostly English and American. He established himself in the Priory of Avon, near Fontainebleau, from 1922.

In 1954, François Mauriac described him as:

Mr. Gurdjieff, the man who brought from the Orient a method for killing the self and for becoming yourself again…

Louis Pauwels, who worked with him, describes his role in his book *Monsieur Gurdjieff*:[33]

Gurdjieff was seen – is still seen by serious thinkers - as a man possessing many different secrets relating to the life of matter, of the spirit, to the laws of the cosmos, etc. He had perhaps acquired that 'principal and absolute knowledge', referred to by the traditionalists and particularly by René Guenon…

---

[33] Page 51

The ABC of the Enneagram

Oscar Ichazo

A son of a high level Bolivian civil servant, Oscar Ichazo was born in 1931. In his twenties he travelled for several years to the Middle East where he was initiated into – among others things – Sufism. He taught at the Institute of Applied Psychology of Santiago, Chile before leading in 1970 an eleven-month course in Arica (Chile), which brought together 50 key people in spiritual development from around the world, including Claudio Naranjo and Alexandro Jodorowski, and where he taught different spiritual development techniques.

Ichazo established the relationship between the nine passions and the diagram. This major discovery made possible – albeit against Ichazo's wishes – the development of the Enneagram in its modern form.

Ichazo developed a theory of enneagons in which he brought together the different phases of the formation of the ego and its liberation. He was the first to teach the Enneagram (diagram + theory of passions) in the West. He founded the Arica school in New York in 1971. The Enneagram is only a part of the Arica teaching, and documents on Arica are not yet in the public domain.

Claudio Naranjo

Naranjo is a Chilean doctor, an honorary faculty member teaching at Harvard and Berkeley, who currently lives in Spain.

He learned about the Enneagram from Ichazo in 1970. He in turn created research teams and established a connection between these passions, the work of Gurdjieff on the one hand, and modern pathologies on the other. He also created a system of panels, which would later be developed by Helen Palmer.

Helen Palmer

Helen Palmer is a teacher of psychology and intuition. She learned about the Enneagram from Claudio Naranjo in 1971. Helen has written five books in the literature of consciousness, including two international bestsellers on the Enneagram, which now appear in 18 foreign translations.

Helen is currently (2003) the subject of a public television documentary "Breaking Out of the Box: Discovering the Enneagram", and together with David Daniels, M.D., co-directs The Trifold School, an organisation that reflects her thirty year commitment to bridging personal and spiritual realities (www.authenticenneagram.com).

Helen already had many years of experience in the field of intuition when she started working with the Enneagram in 1971. Thanks to this experience, she has a rich way of presenting the types. Her major contribution has been to format and teach the material in a safe and living way.

David Daniels, M.D.

David is Clinical Professor, at the Department of Psychiatry and Behavioral Sciences, Stanford Medical School, and is co-founder with Helen Palmer of the Trifold School of Enneagram Studies. With Professor Michael Ray he taught the popular Enneagram and Leadership course at the Stanford Graduate School of Business.

Together with Helen Palmer he has pioneered the Enneagram Professional Training Program through which he has trained hundreds of professionals world wide in use of the Enneagram in fields ranging from business to psychology. He has taught the Enneagram throughout the world since 1988. He is the author of the *Essential Enneagram*, Harper.

Bob Ochs

A Jesuit priest, he was part of Naranjo's work group in San Francisco in 1971. He taught the Enneagram in the context of spiritual development at Loyola University in Chicago to many Christian teachers. Among these was Don Riso, who later founded a school with Ross Hudson.

From the beginning, Bob Ochs was struck by the relationship between the ideas of the higher mental centre of the points Three, Six, and Nine: Hope, Faith, and Love, and certain passages of the Bible[34]. The teaching of Bob Ochs was the starting point for recent developments of the Enneagram in different Christian traditions.

1984, the first book on the Enneagram

It was three students of Bob Ochs: Father O'Leary, Maria Beesing, and Robert Nogoseck, who published the first book on the Enneagram of personality types in 1984, thus breaking the custom of oral transmission

---

[34] The nine ideas of a higher mind centre are, from *Transpersonal Psychologies* by Charles Tart, in order from one to nine: Perfection, Freedom, Hope, Originality, Omniscience, Faith, Conscientious Work, Truth, and Love.

The passages from the New Testament where you find associations with Hope, Faith, and Love are notably in Corinthians Chapter 13, verse 13; Colossians 1, 4-5; Thessalonians 1,3:5,8.

The ABC of the Enneagram

of the Enneagram. This first book caused shock among those who contributed to the development of the system in its recent form. Some thought it was dangerous to popularise such a powerful system. But it was already too late. Oscar Ichazo tried to claim his author's rights, but the case was dismissed. The Enneagram thus passed into the public domain and went round the world in a couple of months. It thus followed the same path as other age-old traditions like the kabbalah, which has recently become accessible to a greater number of people, after remaining secret for centuries, for better or for worse.

The Transpersonal Dimension[35]

We are now going to place the Enneagram in a still more universal context: in the tradition of what Carl Jung called the collective unconscious and which later gave birth to the transpersonal tradition.

For Joseph Campbell[36], myth is:

a dimension which illuminates the conscience by reflecting symbols which come from the unconscious and which help us see deep truths.

Myths are the inner realities of our psyche. They have become more and more recognised as metaphors which help to illuminate the labyrinth of our inner life. They reflect the spiritual potential of each of us.

One of Campbell's main symbols is the circle. It represents our psyche in its entirety. Through the circle, we have a means of creating a link between our personal mythology and the cosmic universe with its tales and legends.

According to Campbell, the function of myth, like that of the Enneagram, is to encourage us to balance and integrate our complementary functions.

The Enneagram as a symbol of unity

The function of the Enneagram is to guide us in our attempt to reconcile the opposing forces inside us. The system of the Enneagram includes the most fundamental principle of Sufism: the concept of unity in multiplicity. This principle recognises in each aspect of everyday life the reflection of a transcendent source that symbolically expresses itself though our human activities.

---

[35] This chapter is much inspired by an article by Joseph Campbell, which appeared in the first issue of *Enneagram Educator* in January 1989. We thank the author and publication for allowing us to reproduce this extract.
[36] *The Power of Myth*, 1991.

In this context, humans are considered to be the microcosm, which is the mirror image of the macrocosm, the Universe. Individuals have inside themselves the ability to choose their own path of integration; they can choose to grow and rise, or stagnate and fall. From that it follows that humans are the final level of creation, and as such, they are the expression of cosmic reality. By each act, each individual recreates creation itself and can thus contribute to advancing the consciousness of the world.

Transpersonal psychology believes that each one of us possesses an essential nature which is different from our acquired personality. One of our objectives as human beings is therefore the construction and fulfilment of the Self. The development of a unique person happens when as individuals we give meaning to our life.

In order to do this, we need reference points, and one of the most powerful ways we can find these for ourselves is by engaging and committing ourselves to the real world. If we don't do this, the alternative is to work on ourselves in the dark, flailing around until some mythological archetype wells up from the psyche to give us a point of reference and guide us.

The Enneagram and mythology

The Enneagram gives us a model and a method for integrating modern and mythological consciousness. By thinking of the circle as a container, the Enneagram affirms the all-encompassing nature of our psyche. The fixations of each type reflect an aspect of everything that disconnects us from the enormous potential of our deep being.

Through its precise descriptions of the emotions and behaviours of each type, the Enneagram gives us a means of identifying our pattern of belief. If you raise the context to another level, the Enneagram addresses the relationship between the personality and other levels of human capability.

Rather than being fixed by our type, the Enneagram invites us to rediscover our hidden potential and consider how we can use it as a means to move to other levels of consciousness. As we have already mentioned, the diagram reflects the Sufi principle of unity in multiplicity, as a means of transcending our fixed position on a particular point.

To return to mythological analogies: the Hero's Journey, whatever it is, is always an experience of going beyond the present. It's about looking further afield. Then an adventure begins, a quest for a new birth that entails separation from our little habits, from our little self, in order to find a new way of being which takes into account the discovery of other points of view.

This type of journey is truly mythological. It involves a quest, danger and setbacks... culminating in the point where all seems lost but where the knot in fact unravels itself, once the integration of opposites is mastered.

The ABC of the Enneagram

Conclusion

This ABC is only a preliminary introduction to the Enneagram personality types, which in itself is only a small part of the Enneagram tradition. More than just a tool, the Enneagram offers us a whole way of looking at things: a compassionate, non-judgemental view, and a state of mind: open to more authenticity, compassion, and tolerance.

The diagram can be used at many levels:
● On the first level, it helps those who are searching for simple keys to self-knowledge to better understand others, and to structure their personal development.
● On the psychological level, the Enneagram is a map of the psyche that enables us to sort out the different forces that make up our inner life.
● On the spiritual level, the Enneagram is used for guiding the path of those who want to make the journey from being an ordinary person to an aware person.

Let us look again at these three levels for one last time.

Knowing yourself and understanding others

As we strive to build our self-knowledge and understanding of others, there are three values which are fundamental:
● Our intuition
● Our sense of humour
● Our certainty of the inner beauty of other people, of their difference from us, and of their uniqueness.

The Enneagram is a system that enables us to structure and develop each of these qualities in ourselves. Its goal is to help us widen our point of view, and each new encounter with another person is a new chance to grow.

On the psychological level

At any given moment, the different forces that drive us are in opposition to each other. These forces can be illustrated by the decision criteria that drive our actions in that moment:

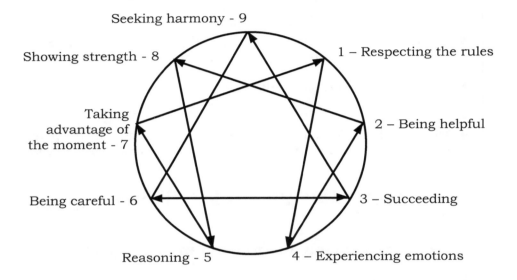

Most of us have silenced the cacophony of opposing forces by focusing, once and for all, on a single one of them. This decision – conscious or not – actually deprives us of a major part of our inner richness.

The ABC of the Enneagram

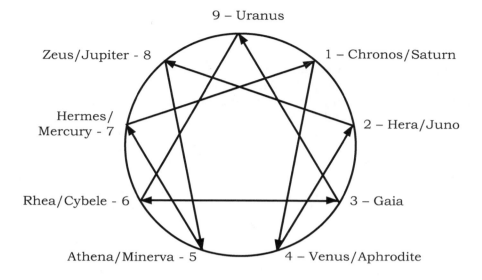

9 – Uranus

Zeus/Jupiter - 8

1 – Chronos/Saturn

Hermes/
Mercury - 7

2 – Hera/Juno

Rhea/Cybele - 6

3 – Gaia

Athena/Minerva - 5

4 – Venus/Aphrodite

These different components of our psyche are found in most mythologies under different names. In Greco-Roman mythology, for example, they are called[37] :

On the psychological level, the Enneagram enables us to:

● Pinpoint which behaviour regularly dominates the others, and thereby name our passion.

In order for our 'nine-horse team' to develop its full potential, we need to get to know and tame each of them. But most of the time, we only use one horse! We therefore need to start by looking around ourselves more widely, in order to rediscover the whole of our potential.

● Harmonise these forces and understand how they interact with each other.

World peace begins with peace inside ourselves. At any given moment, we can choose to be under the influence of our passion and thereby add to the aggressiveness in the air, or to act consciously, in a way that is appropriate to each moment, so that we can be a generator of peace.

---

[37] From the works of Dr Jacques Donnars, Paris. See Bibiography.

On the spiritual level

Through its ancient origins, the diagram offers an important symbolic language. The end goal of spiritual development, the conversion of passion into virtue, is found in many traditions and cultures, and notably in Christianity, Sufism, and Buddhism.

Through self-observation in everyday life, the Enneagram invites us first to notice how much we waste our energy in obsolete defence mechanisms. Then, in stage two, the work of detachment begins: being able to live in the present while being able to put feelings and emotions into perspective. Once this stage is mastered, we can begin the final step towards self-actualisation: being able to channel, then recycle this energy flow into the peace of reconnecting with our essence.

Through the mastery of our inner forces, we can move along the road toward spiritual fulfilment. Fully aware people have succeeded in mastering their instincts, emotions, and thoughts; they are at peace with themselves, with their surroundings and with the universe. It's when we attain this balance that the divine energy can flow freely in us.

To achieve this balance, we must take on the task of resorbing our passion, which is the bottleneck in the divine energy flow. This transformation of the ego in order to reach the higher levels of Being is the existential Quest that we find in so many symbolic images: St. George slaying the Dragon, the Knight searching for the holy Grail, the Alchemist working to transform lead into gold.

And of course, in the end we are talking about ourselves; we are St. George, the Knight, or the Alchemist, if we make the decision to set out on this quest. The Enneagram has already helped us to name our dragon: it's our passion, our dominant type. The Enneagram can also help us as we set out on our journey, as the chart for our voyage, to keep us on course...

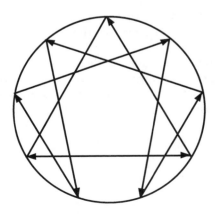

The ABC of the Enneagram

Epilogue

When I started writing this book in 1995, I wanted to share my passion for this tool. I planned to write a simple book, easy to read, to help you to understand that the Enneagram is more than an ordinary typology.

You need to decide whether these goals have been reached in this book. Writing this book convinced me that psychology and what our contemporaries call the spiritual are inseparable. Self-awareness teaches us very quickly that intellectual knowledge about human nature is only an infinitesimal part of understanding the richness and importance of inner life. If only the Enneagram can contribute to bringing together psychology, the spiritual world and science, our civilisation will be infinitely the better for it.

One last word; understanding human nature happens through meeting and getting to know individual men and women. Workshops exist around the world for those who wish to deepen their understanding of the Enneagram by listening to real people. Workshops enable us to go beyond intellectual knowledge of others; through really listening to people we can go beyond external appearances and encounter their living spirit, we have the chance to experience the essence of their being and their inner beauty.

Workshops throughout the world

Association of Enneagram Teachers in the Oral Tradition
1442 A Walnut Street, Suite 377, Berkeley (CA) 94709
Phone : (001) 510 843 76 21
www.enneagramteachers.org   www.authenticenneagram.com

References

Alighieri, D. (1987) *The Divine Comedy*. Paris: Les Éditions du Cerf.
Bedouelle, G. (1991) *Lacordaire*, Le Cerf, Paris
Campbell, J. (1991) *Puissance du Mythe*. Paris: J'ai lu.
Condon, T. (1994) *The Enneagram Movie & video Guide*, The Changeworks, Bend, Oregon, Canada
Daniels, D. & Price, V. (2000) *The Essential Enneagram* New York, Harpers
Frings Keyes, M. (1992) *The Enneagram Relationship Workbook*. Muir Beach, CA: Molystadur Publications.
Gaardner, J. (1991) *Sophie's Verden,* H.Aschenhough & Co, Oslo
Goldberg, M. (1994) article in *Enneagram Monthly,* USA
Kerlys, A. (1992) *La Pierre des Sages*. Toulouse: Terre Blanche.
Malebranche, N. de (1994) , *Oeuvres Complètes,* Tome 1, Vrin, Paris
Mauriac, F. (1995) *Nouveaux Cahiers,* Grasset, Paris
Palmer, H (1996) *L'Ennéagramme en Amour et au Travail*. Montreal: de l'Homme.
Pauwels, L. (1996) *Monsieur Gurdjieff*. Paris: Albin Michel, 1954.
Quirolo, L. (1996) Pythagoras, Gurdjieff and the Enneagram. *Enneagram Monthly*. April/May 1996.
Schuré, E. (1960) *Les Grands Initiés*. Paris: Perrin.
Schwartz, F. (1987) *La Tradition et les Voies de la Connaissance*. Paris: Éditions NADP.
Voltaire (1994) *Dictionnaire Philosophique* Marie-Hélène Cotoni Klincksieck
Webb, K. (1996) *The Enneagram*. Collection Thorsons Principles of. London: Thorsons.

Bibliography

On Pythagoras
Iamblichus
Reference edition on Iamblichus' text:

Main translations and commentaries:
Tr. Gillian Clark (1975) *Iamblichus. On the Pythagorean Life*. Liverpool, UK, Liverpool University Press
Tr. Dillon, J. & Hershbell, J. (1991. *Iamblichus. On the Pythagorean Life*. Atlanta, USA, Scholars Press,
Tr. Brisson, L &. Segonds, A. Ph. (1975) *Iamblichus. On the Pythagorean Life*. Paris: La Roue à Livres, Les Belles Lettres.
Festugière, Father A.J. (1997) Sur une nouvelle edition du *De Vita Pythagorica de Jamblique*. In *Revue des Études Greques*. 50: 470-494.

The ABC of the Enneagram

Other authors in antiquity

Ed. A. Le Bollec. (1981) Clement of Alexandria. *Stomates,* I-XVI, V 57, in *Sources Chrétiennes,* n. 278-279.

Ed. Delatte A. (1922) Diogene Laerce. *Vies et Sentences des Philosophes Illustres,* Book VII, Brussels, 1922, reprinted in 1963.

Ed. Froidefond, C (1988) Plutarch. *Symposium. De Exsilio. Sur Isis et Osiris.* Paris: Les Belles Lettres

Trans. &. Ed. des Places E (1982) Porphyry. *Vie de Pythagore. Lettres à Marcella..* Paris: Les Belles Lettres.

Contemporary authors

Tr Buckert, W. (1972) *Lore & Science in Ancient Pythagoreanism,* Weisheit & Wissenschaft. Cambridge, MA.

Kingsley, P. (1995) *Ancient Philosophy, Mystery and Magic. Empedocles and Pythagorean Tradition.* Oxford.

Levy, Isidore. (1927) *La Legende de Pythagore.* Paris: Champion.

Mattei, J.F. (1993) *Pythagore et les Pythagoriciens.* Collection Que sais-je? n. 2732. Paris : PUF.

Millepierres, F. (1953) *Pythagore, Fils d'Appolon.* Paris: Gallimard.

O'Meara, D. (1989) *Pythagoras Revived.* Oxford: Clarendon Press.

Schuré, E. (1960) *Les Grands Initiés.* Paris: Perrin.

On the Desert Fathers

Bamberger, J.E. (1978). *Cisternician Studies.* Kalamazoo, MI.

Grün, A. (1994) *Der Himmel Beginnt in Dir.* Freiburg in Breisgau: Herderbücherei.

Grün, A.*Geistliche Begleitung bei den Wüstervätern.* Münsterschwarzach, 1992.

Guy, J-C. (1986) *Paroles des Anciens, Apophtegmes des Pères du Désert.* Collection Points. Paris: du Seuil.

Lacarrière, J. (1983) *Les Hommes Ivres de Dieu,* Seuil, Paris

On the Enneagram

In French

Beesing, M: Nagosek, R & O' Leary, P. (1992) *L'Ennéagramme, un Itinéraire de Vie Intérieure.* Paris: Desclée de Brouwer.

Palmer, H. (1995) *L'Ennéagramme.* Geneva: Vivez Soleil.

Palmer, H (1996) *L'Ennéagramme en Amour et au Travail.* Montreal: de l'Homme.

Donnars, Dr. J. (1995) *L'Ennéagramme. Les Neuf Muses et le Transpersonnel.* J. Donnars author-editor. Paris.

In English

Armstrong, James. (1989) The Enneagram. Embodying the Sufi Sense of Unity and the Power of Myth. *Enneagram Educator* 1(Winter 1989).

Bennet, J.G. (1983) *Enneagram Studies.* Coombe Springs, 1974 and Samuel Weiser.

Brady, L. (1994) *Beginning your Enneagram Journey.* Allen, TX: Tabor Publ.

Daniels, D. & Price, V. (2000) *The Essential Enneagram* New York, Harpers

Ebert, A. (1995) Are the Origins of the Enneagram Christian After All? *Enneagram Monthly.* January 1995.

Frings Keyes, M. (1992) *The Enneagram Relationship Workbook.* Muir Beach, CA: Molystadur Publications.

Frings Keyes, M. (1992) *Emotions and the Enneagram.* Muir Beach, CA: Molystadur Publications, 1988, revised 1992.

Hurley, K. & Dobson, T. (1992) *What's My Type?.* San Francisco: Harper.

Hurley, K. & Dobson, T. (1993) *My Best Self: Using the Enneagram to Free the Soul.* San Francisco: Harper.

Naranjo, C. (1992) *Enneatype Structure: Self-Analysis for the Seeker.* Nevada City, CA: Gateway.

Quirolo, L. (1996) Pythagoras, Gurdjieff and the Enneagram. *Enneagram Monthly.* April/May 1996.

Riso, Don R. (1987) *Personality Types: Using the Enneagram for Self-Discovery.* Houghton Mifflin.

Riso, Don R. (1993) *Enneagram Transformations.* New York: Houghton Mifflin.

Riso, Don R. (1987) *Understanding the Enneagram.* Boston: Houghton Mifflin.

Rohr, R. (1990) *Discovering the Enneagram: An Ancient Tool for a New Spiritual Journey.* New York: Crossroad.

Rohr, R. & Ebert, A. (1992) *Experiencing the Enneagram.* New York: Crossroad.

Webb, K. (1996) *The Enneagram.* Collection Thorsons Principles of. London: Thorsons.

Zuercher, S. 1992) *Enneagram Spirituality: From Compulsion to Contemplation.* Notre Dame, IN: Ave Maria Press.

On Sufism

Bakhtiar, L. (1977) *Le Soufisme, Expressions de la Quête Mystique.* Paris: du Seuil.

Lings, M. (1977) *Qu'est-ce que le Soufisme?* Collection Points. Paris: de Seuil.

Arfaoui, H. (1977) *Le Soufisme: Une Profession de Soi en Islam.* Paris: J. Grancher.

On Gurdjieff

Gurdjieff, G.I. (1977) *Rencontres avec des Hommes Remarquables.* Video by the same name produced by Peter Brook. Paris: Du Rocher.

Lefort, R. (1977) *Les Maîtres de Gurdjieff.* Paris: Le Courrier du Livre.

Ouspensky, P.D. (1949) *Fragments d'un Enseignement Inconnu.* Paris: Stock.

Pauwels, L. (1996) *Monsieur Gurdjieff.* Paris: Albin Michel, 1954.

Others

Arvon, H. (1951) *Le Bouddhisme*. Collection Que Sais-Je? Paris: PUF.

Alighieri, D. (1987) *The Divine Comedy*. Paris: Les Éditions du Cerf.

Campbell, J. (1991) *Puissance du Mythe*. Paris: J'ai lu.

Donnars, Dr. J. (1993) *Pour Introduire aux Méditations Transpersonnelles*. J. Donnars author-editor. Paris.

Donnars, Dr. J. (1993) *Méditations Transpersonnelles I: Notre Corps, la Conscience et le Temps*. J. Donnars author-editor. Paris.

Donnars, Dr. J. (1993) *Méditations Transpersonnelles II: Notre Corps, la Conscience et l'Espace*. J. Donnars author-editor. Paris.

Donnars, Dr. J. (1993) *Méditation Transpersonnelle Contemplative*. J. Donnars author-editor. Paris.

Dürckheim, K Graf. (1992) *Le Centre de l'Être*. Paris: Albin Michel.

Grimal, P. (1951) *Dictionnaire de la Mythologie Grecque et Romaine*. Paris: PUF.

Hani, J. (1992) *Mythes, Rites et Symboles*. Paris: Guy Trédaniel.

Kerlys, A. (1992) *La Pierre des Sages*. Toulouse: Terre Blanche.

Naranjo, C. M.D. (1989) *How to Be: Meditation in Spirit and Practice*. Los Angeles: Jeremy P. Tarcher.

Piaget, J. & Inhelder, B. (1967) *La Psychologie de l'Enfant*. Collection Que Sais-Je? Paris: PUF.

Risset, J. (1995) *Dante, une Vie*. Paris: Flammarion.

Sergent, J-C. (1995)*Observer l'Esprit*. Collection Sagesses. Paris: Coleman-Levy.

Schwartz, F. (1987) *La Tradition et les Voies de la Connaissance*. Paris: Éditions NADP.

Tart, C. (1975) *Transpersonal Psychologies*. San Francisco: Harper & Row.

The ABC of the Enneagram